Linguistic Relativity

Linguistic Relativity

An essential guide to past debates and future prospects

FRANCIS JEFFRY PELLETIER
RYAN M. NEFDT

Oxford University Press is a department of the University of Oxford.
It furthers the University's objective of excellence in research, scholarship,
and education by publishing worldwide. Oxford is a registered trade mark of
Oxford University Press in the UK and in certain other countries.

Published in the United States of America by Oxford University Press
198 Madison Avenue, New York, NY 10016, United States of America.

© Oxford University Press 2025

All rights reserved. No part of this publication may be reproduced, stored in a retrieval system, transmitted, used for text and data mining, or used for training artificial intelligence, in any form or by any means, without the prior permission in writing of Oxford University Press, or as expressly permitted by law, by license or under terms agreed with the appropriate reprographics rights organization. Inquiries concerning reproduction outside the scope of the above should be sent to the Rights Department, Oxford University Press, at the address above.

You must not circulate this work in any other form
and you must impose this same condition on any acquirer

CIP data is on file at the Library of Congress

ISBN 9780197799840

ISBN 9780197799833 (hbk.)

DOI: 10.1093/9780197799871.001.0001

Paperback printed by Integrated Books International, United States of America

Hardback printed by Bridgeport National Bindery, Inc., United States of America

The manufacturer's authorised representative in the EU for product safety is Oxford University Press España S.A. of El Parque Empresarial San Fernando de Henares, Avenida de Castilla, 2 - 28830 Madrid (www.oup.es/en or product.safety@oup.com). OUP España S.A. also acts as importer into Spain of products made by the manufacturer.

Contents

Preface   vii
Acknowledgment   xi

1. Basic Linguistic Relativity A Quick Sketch   1

2. Some Historical Antecedents of Linguistic Relativity   5
    2.1 Johann Gottfried von Herder (1744–1803)   8
    2.2 Wilhelm von Humboldt (1767–1835)   14
    2.3 Franz Boas (1858–1942)   19
    2.4 A Miscellany of Reactions to Linguistic Relativity, Independent of Sapir and Whorf (1875–1949)   25

3. Edward Sapir and Benjamin Lee Whorf: Lives, Research, and Whorfianism   29
    3.1 The Life of Sapir (1884–1939)   29
    3.2 Sapir's Linguistic Relativity   34
    3.3 The Life of Whorf (1897–1941)   39
    3.4 Whorf on Linguistic Relativity   43
    3.5 Whorf's (Presumed) Evidence for Relativity   46
    3.6 Reactions and Disputes over the Evidence   48
       3.6.1 Mis- or Non-Understandings of What Whorf Said   49
       3.6.2 Whorf and Malotki on Hopi Time   52
       3.6.3 Greenberg on Whorf   59
    3.7 American Indian Languages: Whorfian Understandings of Structure   61

4. Three Interpretations of Linguistic Relativity   67
    4.1 Is Linguistic Relativity Empirically Testable?   70
    4.2 Constructing (and Evaluating) "Scientific" Relativistic Hypotheses   71

    4.3 *Should* Linguistic Relativity be Empirically Testable?: And If So, How? Emic and Etic Views of Theories of Language and of Its Effects   79
    4.4 Minor Relativism   81
    4.5 Medial Relativism   83
    4.6 Grand Relativism   89

5. Linguistic Relativity and Cognitive Science   92
    5.1 The Linguistic Turn in Philosophy   93
        5.1.1 The Argument from Ordinary Language   96
        5.1.2 Decoloniality and Wiredu's Tongue Dependence   99
    5.2 Linguistics and Relativity   102
        5.2.1 Universal Grammar and Linguistic Diversity   103
        5.2.2 Typology and Diversity   107
    5.3 A Return to Cognition   110
        5.3.1 Lakoff and the Cognitive Commitment   111
        5.3.2 4E Approaches to Cognition   115
    5.4 Large Language Models and Human Cognition   119

6. Conclusion: Whorf and Relativity—Yes? or No?   125
    6.1 No!   125
    6.2 Yes!   126

7. Afterword   127
    7.1 Linguistic Relativity through the Ages   127
    7.2 Whorfianism and Linguistic Relativity   129

Bibliography   133
Index   147

Preface

Linguistic relativity, in one form or another, has fascinated researchers as well as the public imagination for millennia. At its core, it asks us to contemplate the very natures of human thought and language, and what interactions might tie the two together. Some or other view of this connection has informed much of the history of philosophy, psychology, and linguistics. In this book, we delve into the origins of one particular idea that lives like a palimpsest between the lines and pages of some of history's most prominent thinkers, as it continues to lurk within both contemporary thought and future technology.

We don't pretend to solve the relationship between thought, language, and the environment here, but by reviewing one of the most profoundly elusive ideas in contemporary science, we do shed necessary light on a number of related issues – including the transmission of science to the public, the transmogrification of historical figures, the rise of large language models, the replication crisis, folk linguistics, universal grammar, and the intricate interplay between culture and cognition.

Why the historical focus, one might ask. Again, in our present times scholars have faced unprecedented challenges from the media and the public. On the one hand, the public seems to have an insatiable appetite for scientific discovery and innovation. One the other, it has become skeptical of academia and resistant to nuance over splash. There are few better examples of this complex conundrum than the case of Benjamin Lee Whorf and the Sapir-Whorf hypothesis itself. The idea that individual languages determine the bounds of human thought has proven popularly indefatigable. Yet careful scientific reconstruction or precisification yields surprising results. Nothing about so-called Whorfianism or linguistic relativity is straightforward, as we will show. Neither its remit nor its interpretation is as obvious as the intuition behind the idea that the language somehow conditions thought in some measurable manner. Whorf himself has been both celebrated and maligned. In seems to us that neither attitude has been exclusively based in an accurate picture of his actual contributions or claims.

The main thrust of the first part of this book is to concentrate on the particular version offered by Benjamin Lee Whorf in the 1930s–1940s and reactions to that version. However, Whorf's thought has intellectual antecedents that need to be understood, in order to more fully grasp what Whorf proposed. And as well, reactions to Whorf's sometimes oracular pronouncements have led to an industry in trying to empirically verify or falsify his general claims. To these ends we trace one line of thought that preceded Whorf by some 150 years, a line that eventually led to a series of more careful studies of "unusual" languages,[1] starting in the late 1800s. The figures who initiated these studies ... as well as the results that they described about the languages ... had deep influences on Whorf, and we attempt to characterize these interactions.

As we say, Whorf's thoughts about linguistic relativity are only one version of the doctrine. For the doctrine of linguistic relativity more generally holds that the language one has learned as a child will have some influence on the way one characterizes, imagines, views, and interacts with "the world". And there can be many variations on thoughts such as these. Furthermore, these different variations can lead to different conceptions of ways to refute these thoughts; most fervently exhibited in the second half of the twentieth century, lasting through the current years of the twenty-first century. We discuss many of these disputes, including some current studies. And we show how thoughts of linguistic relativity interact with current cognitive science, and with other important applications. We close with a brief characterization of the fundamental assumptions that ultimately distinguish believers from nonbelievers in linguistic relativity.

Before we begin the story of how linguistic relativity came to be identified with the name of Whorf, we need to give the briefest thumbnail sketch–a couple of paragraphs in Chapter 1 – of what that viewpoint is (keeping in mind that we will develop it more fully later) so as to be aware of what is and was the important thrust of the view.

---

[1] Unusual, that is, from the viewpoint of those who studied the European languages.

Linguistic relativity is usually (or at least often) called the *Sapir-Whorf hypothesis*—and also often called just the *Whorf hypothesis* and *Whorfianism*—although the details in many of the works are not really a full, or fully accurate, account of Sapir or of Whorf. For one thing, neither of these authors put forward an explicit hypothesis of the sort we discuss later, nor did either of them adhere to all that has been collected under the banner of the *Sapir-Whorf hypothesis*. The phrase was apparently first coined by Harry Hoijer as a title for a symposium that resulted in the volume of proceedingsHoijer (1954a), although the published version of that volume does not have that phrase in its title (Hoijer's contribution, Hoijer 1954b, does have this title, and very many of the other contributions refer to "the Sapir-Whorf hypothesis").

Most of Whorf's writings that are directly relevant to linguistic relativity of the type to be discussed in this book are gathered in *Language, Thought, and Reality: Selected Writings of Benjamin Lee Whorf*. This title, however, refers to two different volumes: an original volume from 1956 (Carroll 1956b) and what is called a "second edition" (Carroll et al. (2012). The two volumes differ in their choice of "foreword": Stuart Chase wrote the 1956 foreword, but in the 2012 volume the foreword was written by Stephen Levinson (Levinson, 2012), and starts with a note: "This foreword replaces the original by Stuart Chase, whom Whorf viewed as a dubious champion."[2] This new foreword is at pains to rebut various critiques of Whorf (and Whorfianism) that appeared in the years between the two editions. Importantly, this edition also includes (what is called) "The Yale Report", first brought to public attention in Lee, (1996, pp. 251–266), where this report was given a long explanatory exposition. Both Lee (p. 132) and Levinson (p. xix) say this report was written by Whorf alone, despite the appearance of George Trager's name as coauthor. Lee says (p. 132): "Whorf included Trager as co-author in the report because, he said, the parts on phonemics and morphophonemics in Section A were chiefly due to him. The following section . . . Whorf regarded as a joint effort but he took full responsibility for the rest of the document . . . while acknowledging the contribution of discussions with Trager, Hockett,

---

[2] A more lengthy – and less flattering – description of Whorf's attitude toward Chase can be found in Lee, 1996, p. 16, who quotes from various letters of Whorf.

McQuown, Swadesh, Haas, and Voegelin to the development of his own ideas."

Since the works of Whorf as they appeared in the original *Language, Thought, and Reality: Selected Writings of Benjamin Lee Whorf* (as well as Carroll's lengthy introduction, which contains much biographical data about Whorf) appear on different pages of the two volumes, we indicate where they are in both editions of the work, Carroll (1956b) and Carroll et al. (2012), usually in the notes.

In the second part of the book we apply the honed distinctions of the preceding historical and philosophical account to ask probing questions about some of the most influential doctrines of the twentieth century and today. How committed was the linguistic turn in philosophy to linguistic relativity? Is there any argument that can link Chomskyan universalist linguistics to the cross-linguistic anthropological foundations of Sapir and Whorf's era? Do social cognition and the 4E approaches[3] offer some revival of relativity? Is the decolonial turn in contemporary African philosophy driven by ideas of incommensurability and the conceptual causation of language and thought? And lastly, what can the success of large language models tells us about the connections between language and thought?

The style of these chapters will be less historical and comprehensive than the earlier ones, and more suggestive and argumentative. These sections are best treated as vignettes of the still vibrant issues underlying linguistic relativity.

The book as a whole weaves together historical strands, philosophical argument, and linguistic evidence to provide a guide to the endurance of a thought, unshakeable through the ages yet restive enough to constantly escape precise characterization.

Francis Jeffry Pelletier
Edmonton, Alberta, Canada
Ryan M. Nefdt
Cape Town, South Africa

---

[3] Four-E approaches adopt various combinations of enactivism, embodiment, environmental, embeddness. See Shapiro and Spaulding (2024) and especially Newen et al. (2018), with its entries Barrett (2018) and Johnson (2018), among others.

Acknowledgment

This book started life as a portion of the Stanford Encyclopedia of Philosophy entry "The Philosophy of Linguistics", by Barbara Scholz, Francis Jeffry Pelletier, and Geoffrey Pullum. Section 5 of the original 2014 version of that entry was titled "Linguistic Relativity". A request to update the entry (without expansion of the text) led us to delete Section 5, and Pelletier wished to expand those thoughts, include more historical material, and discuss more recent experimental work on the possibility of scientific verification or disconfirmation of linguistic relativity. Very fortunately (according to Pelletier), Ryan Nefdt told Pelletier of his interest in the topic, and together they crafted the current document. Of course, some traces of the original document remain, and we are in debt to the work of Barbara Scholz and Geoffrey Pullum, which at times will still be encountered – at least in spirit. The authors are grateful to Reneé Elio for her enthusiastic support throughout the completion of this project, and especially for her work in the generation of the Index that accompanies it.

1
Basic Linguistic Relativity
A Quick Sketch

At its base, classical linguistic relativity[1] is the view that features of one's language influence or impel or dictate or determine one's individual psychology in its understanding of the natural, physical world. In doing this, they also affect or influence or dictate or determine the "world view" of speakers of the language. And this in turn will influence or dictate or determine the "culture" that the speakers of the language inhabit. Many writers also use the term "relativity" (of thought, concepts, worldviews, etc.) to describe this notion. The terminology of "relativism" in this context was introduced by Edward Sapir (as we will document in §3.2) and also carried forward by Whorf (see §3.4). Our general view of this terminology is that linguistic relativism is a broader notion, covering many and varied types of relativity, whereas Whorfianism is a slight generalization of the variety of relativism Whorf espoused. (But note that Whorf was not entirely specific about all "relativistic" views, so this should probably be taken as meaning some sort of general or broadly applicable notion of relativism.)

But wait a minute! Whorfianism, and linguistic relativity more generally, might be the other way around: some adherents (and some opponents) of linguistic relativity perhaps hold that the "culture" in which children are raised might itself generate or dictate or determine or affect the "worldview" of its members, which in turn might impel— or dictate or determine or cause—not only the individual psychology of the growing child to be of a certain nature but also will thereby make

---

[1] One can also consult Swoyer (2015); Baghramian and Carter (2022) for other "basic accounts". As well, we recommend Levinson (2012, p. x), for a somewhat deeper, six-premise overview of the "central ideas"—as he calls them—of Whorfianism.

the language become suited to expressing or exhibiting or manifesting such a "worldview".

And to make the picture even more muddy: although it is common to claim that linguistic relativity (and Whorf's version in particular) presumes that one's language-type will either cause some cultural features, or will be caused *by* some cultural features, or at least they will in some way or other reflect one another, we note now that Whorf explicitly denied any of these claims. Whorf (1941b) says: "I should be the last to pretend that there is anything so definite as 'a correlation' between culture and language" and to this sentence adds the footnote "We have plenty of evidence that this is not the case. Consider only the Hopi and the Ute,[2] with languages [that] on the overt morphological and lexical level are as similar as, say, English and German. The idea of 'correlation' between language and culture, in the generally accepted sense of correlation, is certainly a mistaken one."

But perhaps they are all partially interwoven in various imaginable ways? And to possibly confuse matters even further, a further distinction is sometime drawn often in the enthnographic and anthropological writings—between "emic" versus "etic" viewpoints. The difference is supposed to be a description or investigation "from the perspective of a member of the group (*emic*)" versus "from the perspective of an observer of the group (*etic*)".[3] An emic-proponent might argue: "it is unrealistic to expect to be able to divorce 'culture' and 'thought' from 'language', in any attempt to independently determine whether there is any relationship between them" (Enfield, 2000, p. 144). On the other hand, an etic-theorist will wish to document some presumed *non*linguistic effects of language cognition and to demonstrate that such effects rely on the language spoken by comparing the behaviours of speakers of different languages. On the other hand, the emic-theorist seeks evidence for or against relativistic effects *within* language use—it is assumed that any such effects are due to *linguistic* categories (like colour terms, metaphors, noun-types [e.g., count vs. mass], politeness terms, etc.), and that these manifest themselves

---

[2] Whose cultures are quite different.
[3] The terms were coined by the linguist Kenneth Pike (1954), although not all current uses of the terms follow the specific senses Pike accorded to them.

in some type or other of *linguistic* behaviour. There is no attempt to test any nonlinguistic type of cognition. The etic-theorist, on the other hand, basically dismisses this intralanguage study as "unscientific" and indeed as irrelevant to linguistic relativism. In some later parts of this book we give a further comparison of these approaches. Many of these places do not explicitly identify as emic or etic, although if the distinction is kept in the reader's mind, it will generally be clear which is being promulgated or dismissed. We more explicitly discuss their different considerations in Chapter 4 here.[4]

As can be seen, there are many possible distinct interpretations of linguistic relativity (and in particular, Whorfianism), even as a basic, foundational starting point. And as might be expected, different strands of Whorfianism might find themselves in a battle over which view is "true Whorfianism". As well, we should be prepared to see critics of linguistic relativism, finding some particular interpretation of some of these oracular pronouncements to be problematic; and dismiss all the other possible understandings with such comments as "Whorfianism ... Ah yes! The undergraduate disease."

---

[4] Even as early as in Carroll's initial "Introduction" to the standard collection of Whorf's papers, there is a recognition of the emic-etic distinction. For example, he remarks:

> It has also been said that it is necessary to find NONlinguistic behaviors which are correlated with the linguistic differences. This would doubtless be desirable, but there is something to be said for being interested in linguistic differences as such, regardless of nonlinguistic behavioral correlates.... Suppose ... we found that, by varying certain environmental conditions, we could produce corresponding changes in the verbal reports made by speakers of a given language. For example, we might be able to find that we could in this way control which of several words (each standing for one of several environmental stimuli) was used as the subject of a sentence reporting the situation. Suppose further that, upon experimenting with speakers of another language, we found it impossible to produce changes in sentence structure corresponding to the varying environmental conditions.... The difference between language behaviors would then be of interest in itself; we would have to conclude that we must take language structure into account in describing the verbal behavior of speakers in selecting the subject component of sentences. If, further, we had some fundamental knowledge about the grammatical meaning of sentence subject, we might be able to make some comparisons of the cognitive processes of the speakers of the two languages. (Carroll, 1956a, pp. 29–30; Carroll, 2012, pp. 36–37)

The way an emic-etic distinction can be used in a "Whorfian theory" will be discussed from various viewpoints in the later chapters of this book.

On a related but more terminological topic, we note that one form of the underlying idea behind linguistic relativism is that speakers of a language will have a "worldview" that is caused by or conditioned by certain of the features of their language (or perhaps the causation is the other way around), and so these worldviews can differ in many important ways from language to language. Conversely, of course, in such a theory the worldviews of similar languages would accordingly need to be similar to one another. Thus Whorf refers to all European and European-derived cultures as "Standard Average European" (SAE). In Whorf's writings SAE is applied both to the "average European" worldview as well as to the "average European" language and the "average European" culture.[5]

---

[5] The terminology was introduced in Whorf (1941b); see Carroll (1956b, p. 138) or Carroll et al. (2012, p. 178) for Whorf's actual remarks.

2
Some Historical Antecedents of Linguistic Relativity

There are many discussions of historical antecedents of linguistic relativism (whatever that should turn out to be), including both the philosophical background and ethnological topics; we mention a number of such histories in the historical parts of this book. In this chapter, we discuss only a few of the historical antecedents, and suggest various places where this topic is further discussed. But again, a full discussion of all the possible historical predecessors is not envisaged or even possible in a short summary, as we view the historical part of this book to be.

If one were to search with wide imagination for antecedents to (some of the parts of) linguistic relativism, one might come up with, say, Hermogenes and a view that "names have no natural connection with reality" and are given purely as a result of social convention; social convention of course varying from society to society. This might not be exactly any of the many forms adopted by current relativists, but does certainly seem to fit the general line of thought.[1] Or one might think of "Buddhist semioticians" as in Barthes (1983) and Rambelli (2013). Or one might think of John Locke's (1689) discussion of the origin of words in Book III of his *Essay Concerning Human Understanding*.[2]

However, we will restrict ourselves by looking only at one early example of a philosophical movement from the seventeenth to eighteenth centuries that is commonly mentioned as a precursor of, or an early form of, or as giving the philosophical foundations for, linguistic relativity. This is the German anti-Kantian movement, or

---

[1] For discussion of Hermogenes (also Cratylus), see Meßer (2020).
[2] "Words... by constant and familiar use... charm men into notions far remote from the truth of things." *Essay* III.10.16.

more accurately, the anti-critical-period-of-Kant movement, which was occasioned by the publication of Kant's *Critique of Pure Reason*. The person usually cited as the originator of this resistance to Kant is Johann Herder,[3] although various commentators have pointed to Herder's correspondence and interactions with others, who perhaps were chronologically equal or even prior. We here, nevertheless, start with Herder, and use him as our only touchpoint of the alleged German anticipation of linguistic relativism. Herder was a philosopher, and so his thoughts are of an a priori nature. Of course, like any educated European of the time, he was knowledgable about the European languages. But his argumentation did not take the form "an examination of languages X and Y shows that . . ."

As a consequence, we think that this strand of anti-Kantianism cannot realistically be said to be an anticipation of Whorfianism, partially because it is not based on language features that are radically different from SAE and partially because it is aimed only at arguing against the Kantian critical period view that human cognition is founded by innate concepts and categories. As we will remark later in this book (§6, where we discuss the fundamental requirements for linguistic relativity) this might embody one type of necessary condition for a Whorfian viewpoint, but is not sufficient.

Following that, we look at two more direct antecedents of linguistic relativity from the realm of anthropological linguistics (ethnography): Wilhelm von Humboldt and Franz Boas. The writings of these thinkers attracted the attention of a number of scholars, both ethnographical and philosophical. Their argumentation is not that of Herder, but rather based on examination of other cultures and languages. Many of their claims seem sympathetic to linguistic relativity, although they are rather far from endorsing what many have claimed to be the distinctive features of Whorfianism, and they do not address the sort of issue that German philosophical tradition emphasized. And while they do remark on – and even emphasize – the differences between SAE and other languages that they studied, they do not seem

---

[3] As we point out in §2.1, of the two works that are traditionally said to embody Herder's anti-Kantian stance, one was written long before Kant's critical period and the other was a direct response to the *Critique of Pure Reason*.

to commit to specific views concerning the relations that might hold among "language vs. worldview vs. culture". Nor do they really remark on how these are "radically different from" SAE – at least, not in the ways that Whorfianism emphasizes and draws its conclusions from. It seems that putting these aspects together, and calling it *linguistic relativity* was first done by Sapir in his (1924, p. 155). (It seems to be Sapir's view in this article that language serves as a "filter" for communication about the world. We cite his remarks and discuss them in §3.2.) Despite this fact, though, the investigations and viewpoints of Humboldt and Boas are nonetheless an important background to understanding the resulting Whorfianism version of linguistic relativity in the twentieth century. We follow this ethnographical discussion with some reaction of various scholars in §2.4 – philosophers, linguists, mathematicians, and others – to these claims, made during the times prior to the rise of Whorfianism in the 1940s. Some of these reactions suggest an early appreciation of (some forms of) linguistic relativity.

In Chapter 3 we give short accounts of the lives of Sapir (§3.1) and Whorf (§3.3). We then cite the places where Sapir (§3.2) and Whorf (§3.4) describe their (somewhat different) understandings of linguistic relativity. In the case of Whorf, we present a selection of his best known pieces of evidence for his Whorfianism in §3.5, sometimes with a further explanation of how these thoughts fit in with some current accounts. And finally, in §3.6, we discuss the reactions, disputes, and acrimony over Whorf's thoughts in this area. We do this at least partially to counter the many claims by certain anti-Whorfian scholars that Sapir's and Whorf's analyses are sloppy or question-begging or amateurish. It will be seen that their actual descriptive work is solid, and if there are errors, they involve matters of certain theoretical constructions that are used to explain the data. And these theory-laden constructions are not at all silly and without merit, even in those few cases where they have been supplanted by more modern theoretical moves.

Chapter 4 examines the extent to which Whorfianism – or indeed *any* version of linguistic relativity – can deliver anything at all like a scientifically examinable hypothesis. Here we look at various attempts that have been described, and return to a discussion of the emic-etic distinction applied to this realm, where we distinguish a "grand" from a "minor" version or dimension of understanding Whorfianism (not to be conflated with the well-known but different and overworked "strong" versus "weak" Whorfianism). After this we turn our attention to various academic areas that have important insights to bring to the discussion of linguistic relativity, particularly cognitive science. We then discuss a number of academic (and social) areas where linguistic relativism has found some important applications. In Chapter 5, we delve into contemporary cognitive science and find linguistic relativity underlying a number of theories and frameworks, from Chomskyan linguistics to natural language processing, under different guises. In fact, we show that questions surrounding relativity are not only applicable to contemporary linguistics but can offer unique insight into the current philosophical discussions on meaning in large language models. We close with an overview of what we think are the two central presuppositions or preconditions that are relevant to acceptance or denial of linguistic relativism. One is philosophical-cum-cognitive in nature and the other is linguistic-cum-anthropological in nature.

2.1 Johann Gottfried von Herder (1744–1803)

As we have indicated, an often-mentioned philosophical antecedent of linguistic relativity is Johann von Herder.[4] Herder was perhaps foremost among the philosophers opposed to the position taken by Kant in his *Critique of Pure Reason*.[5] The two main documents Herder wrote in this regard were his 1772 essay titled (in English) *Treatise on the Origin of Language* and a later work, his 1799 *Understanding and Experience: A Metacritique of the Critique of Pure Reason*. Of course,

---

[4] Of course, there are others we could have cited, for example Johann Georg Hamann (1730–1788), who is sometimes thought to be a touchstone for Herder, given the extended correspondence they had. But we think Herder is a better starting point for this historical train of thought. Interested readers might consult Griffith-Dickson (2022) for a survey of Hamann's thought.

[5] See the entry in the *Stanford Encyclopedia of Philosophy*: Forster (2022). Herder's relevant views can be found in §§4 and 5 of this entry. See especially also §1 of the Supplement to the Herder entry, https://plato.stanford.edu/entries/herder/supplement.html#HerRolBir. For a more general account of the life of Herder see Clark (1955); for works more concerned with Herder as a precursor to Whorf see (for example) Penn (1972); Joseph (1996); Deutscher (2010); Allan (2010).

the former piece appeared prior to Kant's critical period, and so is not really a reaction to the *Critique of Pure Reason*, but nonetheless it sets the stage for a number of the German writers who reacted against Kant's later works and, as well, places the latter work of Herder into the appropriate context.

Herder's 1772 work was his entry to the Berlin Academy's Prize essay contest. In 1769 the topic was "If mankind were left to their natural faculties, would they be in a position to invent language? And by what means will they achieve this invention by themselves?" The dominant position, at least in Germany, seems to have been that language was given or revealed to man by God. Other theories held that mankind was without language, but some men recognized the inconvenience of this and got together to "invent" a method of communication (a view sometimes attributed to Rousseau). A further theory (perhaps best developed by Condillac) had it that language was the outcome of the reflexes that get expressed as cries when impacted by the environment, and that vocabulary growth went hand in hand with these experiences. And Herder was set to give an alternative account that made language acquisition be due to the "nature of humans" and the "natural state they find themselves in". This essay was written during December 1771, and mailed before Christmas that year to the Berlin Academy secretary. It was 166 pages long, leading most scholars to believe that Herder had thought about the topic for many years before the announcement of the Berlin Academy Prize for 1772 – which he won.

Edward Sapir's MA thesis (1905, published as Sapir, 1907), was about this essay of Herder's. Although it contains Herder's name in its title, it has seemed to some not to provide much discussion of Herder's idea of language shaping one's thought (as, e.g., Joseph 1996, pp. 367–368, puts it). According to Joseph, Sapir identifies the main problem behind Herder's investigations as Herder's claims of an evolution of languages leading to European-style languages, whereas Sapir instead argues that all of the world's languages have equal aesthetic potentials and grammatical complexity. And Joseph says that Sapir ends with a call for a study of all existing stocks of languages, in order to determine the most fundamental properties of language. But we might note that Sapir also recognized the "remarkable intuitive power [with which] Herder grasped some of the most vital points both in psychology and language." Of course Sapir was not favourably disposed towards the way that "the philosophers of the eighteenth century, [relied] very heavily on pure reason unfettered by hard facts" and wonders that they "could be so cocksure of the solution of certain linguistic problems as Herder seems to have been" (Sapir 1907, p. 136).

And although it is true that Sapir held the equality or independence of all languages, perhaps Joseph's comment is nonetheless too quick with Sapir's actual account. For Sapir admired very many aspects of Herder's essay, for example the way "Herder attempted, as much as possible, to make use of what linguistic material was at hand in the verification of his theories" and that the essay was "remarkable ... for the systematic development of the theme and for clearness of exposition." And Sapir finds it worth mentioning that Herder "succeeded so well in demonstrating the human origin of language" as opposed to insisting on its being a "gift of God". Sapir also credits Herder with recognizing the facts that there are different languages ... some so different[6] that they cannot all be "given once for all by God", and that Herder uses various "psychological truisms" that show how different languages reflect the environmental and cultural differences that speakers inhabit. (For example, Herder also considers how languages have synonyms ... he mentions Arabic as having "two hundred words for *snake* and about a thousand for *sword*" ... and argues that this shows the control of culture and environment on linguistic development. As Herder puts it, "language is rich in synonyms; alongside of real poverty it has the most unnecessary superfluity. God would not supply such a surfeit of alternatives.")

Sapir, while finding much to admire in Herder's approach in his analysis of language and languages, cautions us not to expect any "modern" insights into language analysis:

> We should never forget that Herder's time-perspective was necessarily very different from ours. While we unconcernedly take tens and

---

[6] Sapir cites Herder as considering "the oriental, by which he [Herder] means one or two Semitic, dialects" and the "languages of primitive peoples as being more 'original' than our modern vernaculars".

even hundreds of thousands of years in which to allow the products of human civilization to develop, Herder was still compelled to operate with the less than six thousand years that orthodoxy stingily doled out. To us the two or three thousand years that separate our languages from the Old Testament Hebrew seems a negligible quantity, when speculating on the origin of language in general; to Herder, however, the Hebrew and the Greek of Homer seemed to be appreciably nearer the oldest conditions than our vernaculars – hence his exaggeration of their *Ursprünglichkeit*. The supposedly "primitive," or rather "original," character of the languages of the savages was due to a very natural, though, unfortunately, on the whole erroneous, conclusion from *à priori* considerations. (Sapir, 1907, p. 117)

Once Kant published the *Critique of Pure Reason*, Herder was quick to respond negatively, with his *Understanding and Experience: A Metacritique of the Critique of Pure Reason* even though he had been Kant's student in the 1760s. Herder had a skepticism about metaphysics and had a generally empiricist outlook, especially when it came to the content of our concepts, thinking that all concepts come from sense perception and therefore apperception of this content must precede the concept thus formed. Herder believes that ideas, with which reason operates, cannot be distinguished from words; so that a person (or a people) has no idea for which it has no word. Hence, reason functions only through language . . . and language is in turn ultimately derived from sensation. Stam (1980, p. 254-255) describes Herder's (and Hamann's) general attack on Kant this way: "their attack centered around two broad points: first, Kant's adherence to a discredited faculty psychology; second, Kant's failure to understand the role of language. . . . [Herder and Hamann claimed that] Kant failed to take account of language and the role it plays in the shaping of perceptions, the formation of judgments, and the construction of ideas. This neglect leaves Kant open to a charge which would be devastating to the arguments of the *Critique*, namely that the *a priori* forms of perception and of judgment and the ideas of reason themselves are all linguistically derived categories".

One can see that this general framework might lead to something akin to Whorfianism, although it seems clear that Herder did not adopt that viewpoint fully.[7]

Quite a few of the German philosophers reacted in opposition to this phase of Kant's work, expressed in his *Critique of Pure Reason*, with its presumption of "innate ideas" and the uniformity of human cognition to arrive at a necessary commonality of all humans. In the end, however, these opponents were effectively removed from the philosophical stage by the pro-Kantian forces. Nonetheless, we can get one direction of the anti-Kantian movement in philosophy by looking at some of the more lasting thoughts of Herder. In Penn's view (1972, p. 11], Herder, as well as Humboldt, Sapir, and Whorf, advocated the view that one's thought depends on one's language and that this "extreme view" is "... in a sense necessary to Western thought – necessary to free us of the notion of innate ideas, e.g., Kant's categories. Linguistic relativity is seen as an antidote to the a priori assumption of innate categories of thought and a God who created language, just as the notion of the cultural relativity of values has been necessary to free us of the conviction that there is a pre-ordained ... moral law to which all are subject".

In the context of the Kantian development of Categories of Thought, an issue central to these earlier developments of "proto-Whorfian thought" (and to many of the more recent accounts) concerns the temporal – or, perhaps, conceptual – linkage between cognition and language:

- Is it possible to have concepts without language?
- Is all thinking done in a language (even if this is "just" a mental language)?

It has seemed to many theorists that linguistic relativity is committed to the view that all thinking is in a language. For, if not, then language *could not* determine or dictate or ... one's concepts and

---

[7] Kant defenders have objected to Herder's *Metacritique* (as it is usually called) on a variety of grounds, and while this is not the place to discuss this controversy, the interested reader might consult Menges (1998); Sikka (2007). It is also not feasible to discuss, in this brief historical survey, enough of Kant's views on thought and language to see whether, or if so how, Herder's position is a viable alternative. For relevant discussion of Kant's views, see Forster (2012), for example.

worldview. Herder put it this way: "without language man can have no reason, and without reason no language." Allan (2010, p. 229) says that "Herder apparently believed that thought needs language, as did Leibniz, as did the German Romantic Johann G. Hamman (1730–1788); subsequently Chomsky (in Chomsky, 1975, 1980) reached a similar conclusion." A footnote to this remark of Allan's continues: "by way of contrast,[8] Humboldt, Sapir, and Whorf all believed that thought is shaped by language... Saussure too." Although there does seem to be a contrast between the two positions, it is not very clear what exact claim is being made in contrasting *thought needs language* with *thought is shaped by language*.

Relevant to Herder's presaging linguistic relativity, one should in particular consult the discussions in work by (Clark (1955, pp. 384–412) and Stam (1980, pp. 244–254), of Herder's *Metacritique*. Clark remarks (p. 405) that "Herder's chief result in the *Metacritique* is the identification of thought with language", and cites Herder as saying "What is *thinking*? *Inward speaking*;... Speaking is thinking aloud." This view is very often claimed to be a consequence of Whorfianism – sometimes approvingly, sometimes as a critique.

A commonly cited example of Herder's from this document is explained by Clark (1955, p. 410), who also discusses further relevant works of Herder. The following comment concerns an example from Herder's *Treatise on the Origin of Language* of 1772: "[Herder] does not believe that... the words 'sheep,' 'mouton,' and 'Schaf' have any organic or necessary relation to the animal thus designated. But he does mean that for a native speaker of English, French, or German the linguistic connotations will invariably affect the structure of consciousness so far as the semantic field is concerned. Furthermore, the syntactical peculiarities of each language will be regarded by a native speaker of it as components of reality itself – and indeed they are that".

A conclusion to this very brief description of the German anti-Kantian movement seems to have two aspects:

- The main thrust of their argumentation was to assert that, while external audible stimuli can give rise to mental sensations, it is the recognition, by a person, of a "habitual association" among similar stimuli that gives rise to a "linguistic concept" where the

[8] Contrasting Herder, Leibniz, Hamman, and Chomsky with the following.

audible stimulus becomes the "name" of the concept. And this concept and its name thus becomes associated with the observed cause of the stimulus.

- They did *not* emphasize (and maybe didn't see) that speakers of different languages could (and in fact *do*) differ in truly fundamental ways from one another, but they instead thought that since humans were motivated by the same desires and needs, and had the same abilities to use their intelligence to meet these desires and needs, the different languages would not be different enough to justify the sort of radical results that Whorfianism (and linguistic relativity more generally) predicts.

The second of these aspects is at least partially due to the fact that their knowledge of the types of vast differences that can and do exist between languages was limited by their concentration on the SAE languages.

The philosophical movement lost out: even the anti-Kantian philosophers for the most part instead took positions on topics other than a philosophy of language which would favour (what we now call) linguistic relativity.

The next Whorf-like force was from (what should seem to philosophers) an unlikely source: linguistic anthropology, or ethnography.

2.2 Wilhelm von Humboldt (1767–1835)

Of the early forces that drew attention to non-SAE languages, the most important was Wilhelm von Humboldt, the elder brother of the better-known Alexander von Humboldt.[9] But we start with a cautionary note from Mueller-Vollmer and Messling (2017, opening paragraph):[10] "it is quite misleading to associate the term "Humboldtian linguistics" or "Humboldtian philosophy of language" with any

---

[9] For accounts of the linguistic philosophy of other philosophers of the general time frame, see Forster (2010a, b).

[10] For von Humboldt's views on language, see especially §§ 1.3, 1.4, and 4–7 of their SEP entry. And consult this entry's very extensive bibliography, especially the section "Secondary Literature: Philosophy and Linguistics".

one specific direction, for example with the Whorfian thesis of "linguistic relativity" or with Chomsky's opposite notion of a universalist "generative grammar" because these tend to ignore other equally or more important dimensions of Humboldt's work".

Although this is certainly true, the fact of the matter is that there *is* a seemingly Whorfian strand to a certain direction of Humboldt's thought, and it was at least partially that strand that drew a number of later ethnographers to emphasize their own Whorfian views. We will show a little later the effect that Humboldt's interest in the study of non-European languages and cultures had on the ethnographic communities within Germany (especially) but also on other European scholars, including influences felt even in USA-authored linguistics books written in the nineteenth century. Basically, we think that Humboldt's interest in non-SAE languages sparked what is a precondition of linguistic relativity: an interest and study of languages which are the primary data that might support or confirm linguistic relativity. However, we do not see that Humboldt specifically drew the characteristic Whorfian conclusions about different conceptual schemes or worldviews from his studies. But before we get into that, we lay out some of the trends that can be found in Humboldt's best-known work, which is known informally as *The Kawi Introduction* (von Humboldt, 1836).

Wilhelm von Humboldt led a life of financial ease, and used his time to master languages. Apparently, the first of the non-SAE languages he encountered was Basque, having traveled to the Basque Country in 1801. He added languages of Central America from the grammars (by missionaries) that were sent to him by his brother Alexander, and then went on to study (as Hans Aarsleff puts it)[11] "the following groups of languages, roughly in this order and citing only the most important: The Sanskrit, North-American Indian, Chinese, Polynesian, and Malayan languages until he finally around 1830 made the Kawi (or Kavi) language the center both of his cosmos and of the large work that was designed to display the ultimate synthesis of his philosophy of language."

---

[11] In the very interesting and very detailed introduction to von Humboldt (1836) that he wrote (Aarsleff, 1988). See also the chapter "Wilhelm von Humboldt and the Linguistic Thought of the French *Idéolgues*," in Aarsleff (1982a).

Aarsleff's introduction to the work of von Humboldt (1836) makes it clear just how consumed Humboldt was with language, with language-learning, and with the relation between "national character" and the language of the relevant nation. He was also, however, a self-admitted terrible writer. He tended to go into details that detracted from his overall narrative and, more importantly (so far as his publications went), he was self-confessedly unable to revise or rewrite parts of works that had consumed him for some time. Instead, he claimed that he required starting anew and rewriting the entire document, even when the problem that his friendly confidants had suggested was only that this or that passage was "too turgid" or "needed further explanation." As a result, much of his work was left uncompleted. And his proposed grand opus, *On the Kawi Language on the Island of Java*, which had an "introductory essay" titled "The Diversity of Human Language-Structure and Its Influence on the Mental Development of Mankind," was not completed while he lived. This introductory essay – a book-length work of its own – was completed by his brother, Alexander, with the acknowledged (in its preface, written by Alexander) help of various friends and acquaintances of Wilhelm. This completion was accomplished remarkably quickly and resulted in Wilhelm's best-known work, which was published within a year of his death. The work is usually known as *The Kawi Introduction* (rather than its official title), and we cite it from the 1988 translation by Peter Heath (in von Humboldt, 1836). The remainder of *On the Kawi Language on the Island of Java* – some 2,000 pages – was published in three volumes between 1836 and 1839.[12]

The following are some relevant quotations from von Humboldt's *Kawi Introduction*, giving the flavour of his experiences with the various exotic languages.

> ... [The diversity of languages rests on their form, and the latter is most intimately connected with the mental attitudes of nations ... (von Humboldt, 1836, p. 54)

> Language is the formative organ of *thought*. *Intellectual activity*, entirely mental, entirely internal, and to some extent passing without

---

[12] For an interesting (and enthusiastic!) description of the latter work, see Weissbach (1999).

trace, becomes, through *sound*, externalized in speech and perceptable to the senses. Thought and language are therefore one and inseparable from each other. (von Humboldt, 1836, p. 54)

... There resides in every language a characteristic *world-view*. ... The entire language steps in between [a speaker of the language] and the nature that operates, both inwardly and outwardly, upon him.... Every language draws about the people that possessed it, a circle whence it is possible to exit only by stepping over at once into the circle of another one. To learn a *foreign language* should therefore be to acquire a new standpoint in the world-view hitherto possessed, and in fact to a certain extent is so, since every language contains the whole conceptual fabric and mode of presentation of a portion of mankind. But because we always carry over, more or less, our own world-view, and even our own language-view, this outcome is not purely and completely experienced. (von Humboldt, 1836, p. 60) Man lives with objects mainly ... even exclusively ... in the way that language leads him to. (von Humboldt, 1836, p. 60)

Now, everyone uses language to express his most particular individuality; for it always proceeds from the individual, and each uses it primarily for himself alone. Yet it suffices everyone, insofar as words, however inadequate, fulfil the urge to express one's innermost feelings. Nor can it be claimed that language, as a universal medium, reduces these differences to a common level. It does indeed build bridges from one individuality to another, and is a means of mutual understanding; but in fact it enlarges the difference itself, since by clarifying and refining concepts it produces a sharper awareness of how such difference is rooted in the original cast of mind. The possibility of serving to express such diverse individualities seems, therefore, to presuppose in language itself a perfect lack of character, with which, however, it can by no means be reproached. It actually combines the two opposing properties of dividing itself, as one language in the same nation, into an infinity of parts, and as such an infinity, of uniting itself, as one language of a particular character, against those of other nations. (von Humboldt, 1836, p. 151)

Every language receives a specific originality through that of the nation, and has on the latter a uniformly determining reverse effect. (von Humboldt, 1836, p. 152)

Allan (2010, p. 237), emphasizing the same interpretation of von Humboldt, cites many of these same quotations and also gives some further citations from other works of von Humboldt.

> Every language sets certain limits to the spirit of those who speak it; it assumes a certain direction and, by doing so, excludes many others.[13]
>
> The diversity of languages is not a diversity of sounds and signs but a diversity of the views of the world.[14]

He follows them with the remark "here we see that Humboldt is truly an originator of the so-called 'Sapir-Whorf', 'Whorfian' or 'linguistic relativity' hypothesis. Humboldt judged that because language and thought are intimately connected, the grammatical differences between languages are manifestations of different ways of thinking and perceiving. The structure of language affects perceptual processes and also the thought processes of speakers. Language mediates worldview such that different world-views correlate with different language structures that no sole individual can change; consequently languages are stable organic wholes."

Shall we agree with Allan that Humboldt is the true originator of the Sapir-Whorf hypothesis (or at least, of something very much like it)? Or shall we revert to the common opinion (among history-of-philosophy-of-language scholars) that Herder (in conjunction with other philosophers of the era, such as Hamann) is the true founder of the movement?[15] Or shall we perhaps say none of these fully embraced the necessary ingredients of Whorfianim? We have already remarked that Herder and the other German anti-Kantians held to this pair of positions: (a) they denied that languages were in some mysterious way a "gift from God" but held rather that individuals learned them by experiences, and (b) they denied that there was some innate language-learning capacity that would generate what is (essentially) the same

---

[13] Allan (2010, p. 237) cites this as from von Humboldt's *Introduction to General Linguistics*, an unpublished work of 1810–1811.

[14] Allan cites this from Trabant (2000, p. 25), who in turn says it occurs in "Humboldt's first academic discourse (1820)" as an outline of a program of linguistic research. Allan, however, gives a slightly different translation from the one by Trabant.

[15] For example, in Haß ler (2006, p. 7).

language in every human being. These are certainly claims that are friendly to linguistic relativity. But they nonetheless did not have an appreciation of the true differences that can occur between languages, since their acquaintance with languages was basically limited to the Indo-European (= SAE) languages. So, although we acknowledge the presence of a Whorfian-friendly background philosophy, it seems too much of a stretch to call them real linguistic relativists.

But what about von Humboldt? One thing that might hold back our acknowledging him to be the originator is that, despite his acquaintance with a variety of languages, courtesy of his brother's sending lexical and grammatical sketches produced by missionaries, the fact is that he had no *experience* of the belief systems of these peoples, and no clear empirical (or even impressionistically nonempirical) way to judge whether the "World-Views" and the "Culture" (and any other constructions that linguistic relativity appeals to) matched up or differed from the languages of the various peoples that the grammars were describing. And this is just as much a central part of linguistic relativity as is the viewpoint that the languages themselves seem to be radically different from SAE languages.

So again, it seems wrong to identify von Humboldt as a true Whorfian. We would want him to have more direct experience and information about the "World Views" of the actual speakers of these languages, before we can say that he really adopted the linguistic relativist perspective.

2.3 Franz Boas (1858–1942)

Franz Boas received a PhD in physics in 1881 at the University of Kiel, while also studying geography. During his military service (1882–1883), he pondered and published on issues about the relationship between psychology and the physical world, and apparently thought of evaluating this relationship by looking closely at a case of a very stark world and the resulting psychological (and linguistic) relations that might be engendered. To that end, and encouraged by his geography professor at Kiel, he prepared a grant proposal to spend a year with the Inuit of Baffin Island (Canada). In 1883 he lived on the island and closely followed the life of an Inuit group for a year, focussing on native migration patterns.[16] This resulted in his 1886 Habilitationschrift, *Baffin Land*, and a little later the (English) 1888 report *The Central Eskimo*, published by the Bureau of American Ethnology.[17]

After the Baffin expedition, Boas took a position at the Royal Ethnological Museum of Berlin in 1885 and was introduced to languages and culture of the First Peoples of the coastal British Columbia in western Canada. And after completing his Habilitationschrift, Boas embarked on a three-month trip to British Columbia. In 1887 the journal *Science* gave him a paid assistant editorship, and he decided to return to North America permanently; in 1889 he was appointed to head a new Department of Anthropology at Clark University (in Worcester, Massachusetts). In 1896 he moved to Columbia University and negotiated the gathering of all the various anthropologically oriented professors into one department, which became the first American PhD program in anthropology.

In the nineteenth and early twentieth centuries, one of the main disputes in anthropology/ethnology concerned the true underlying causes of the differences among the different groups of people: their anatomies, their physiologies, their mental characteristics. Certainly the groups living in different places around the globe were different in these various ways, and a main focal question was: What is the explanation of these differences? The generally assumed explanation seems to have been some sort of "evolutionary story": different societies evolve more or less slowly, but ultimately aim at the same goal. To this view's proponents, the aim of the then-current cultural evolution was to be like European culture(s) (or sometimes more specialized, such as German or French): not, of course, that this was a conscious goal, but rather it was the result of some force of the human social nature. In some similar way, peoples around the world were evolving

---

[16] Boas spent the winter of 1883–1884 in the Cumberland Sound area of Baffin Island, and during the spring and summer of 1894 he crossed the Cumberland Peninsula, visiting various Inuit communities along the coast of the Davis Strait.

[17] See Boas and Müller-Wille (1998) for the journals and field notes; and Cole and Müller-Wille (1984), Knötsch (1993), and Cole (1999) for further information and reflections on the "early Boas".

towards some particular goal (again, the goal was assumed to be European) or might die from "natural causes" (an unfulfilled attempt at evolving, so to speak).

Boas railed against both sides of this story: so far as the physical differences go, he argued and indeed empirically showed that the major explanations were the peoples' environments, their diets, and their general worldly life. His 1911 *The Mind of Primitive Man*, as well as Boas (1912a, b) emphasize that although (e.g.) cranial size and height are inherited traits, diet and other environmental aspects cause changes that are expressed over time and generations. The results of Boas's studies and writings, as well as his public advocacy, form a newer type of "cultural equality": the biological, cultural, and linguistic features of any group of people are the result of historical developments that include both cultural and noncultural forces. Hence the particular culture and environment in which an individual finds himself or herself will structure that individual's specific appearance, health, attitudes, and behavior. Thus Boas outlined a theory of *cultural* relativism, which held each culture had its own historical trajectory, and that the beliefs, values, categories, and customs of a culture should be understood on that culture's own terms. In this he was opposing some sort of "cultural evolution", whereby all cultures aimed towards the same end, and proposing that some of the current cultures were (much) further than others along this trajectory towards an ultimate end. One way that he put his view was this:

> ... anatomical type,[18] language, and culture have not necessarily the same fates; that a people may remain constant in type and language, and change in culture; that it may remain constant in type, but change in language; or that it may remain constant in language, and change in type and culture ... a classification based primarily on type alone will lead to a system which represents more or less accurately the blood-relationships of the people, which do not need to

---

[18] By "anatomical type" Boas means such measures as typical height, general size, skin colour, head shape, and so on. The point of this paragraph seems to be that any combination of these general features of a typical member of some group of people can be associated with any type of language and any type of culture – none being particularly any better than the other possibilities.

coincide with their cultural relationships; and that in the same way classifications based on language and culture do not need at all to coincide with a biological classification. (Boas, 1911, p. 133)

Besides these remarks on culture and physical development Boas had many things to say about the nature of language that presaged and influenced both Sapir and Whorf. This chain of influence is not surprising, since Sapir was a student of Boas, and Whorf studied under Sapir.[19] We mention here just a few of the more commonly cited influences for the view that language plays a role in shaping thought. Of course, Boas thought, all languages have means to classify experiences and to group various instances of them under the same class; but he also thought that different languages can (and do) make these classifications differently.

> ... The groups of ideas expressed by specific phonetic groups show very material differences in different languages, and do not conform by any means to the same principles of classification. ... Thus it happens that each language, from the point of view of another language, may be arbitrary in its classifications; that what appears as a single simple idea in one language may be characterized by a series of distinct phonetic groups in another. (Boas, 1911, pp. 145–147)

> The whole classification of experience among mankind living in different forms of society follows entirely distinct lines.... the principles of classification which are found in different languages do not by any means agree. (Boas, 1911, p. 198)

In Boas (1911, sec. 2) we find examples of this from a variety of different languages. The idea was that a given experience would be differently rendered in various languages, or sometimes, a set of experiences would be differently grouped in different languages. His most (in)famous example concerns the various words in Eskimo relating to snow:[20]

---

[19] Despite some later possible alienation between Sapir and Boas. See Darnell (1990, pp. 279–287, 379) for hints of this.
[20] Martin (1986), is a short "research note" in *American Anthropologist* that takes issue with the popular use of Boas's example as a starting point for some arbitrarily

SOME HISTORICAL ANTECEDENTS   23

To take again the example of English, we find that the idea of WATER is expressed in a great variety of forms: one term serves to express water as a LIQUID; another one, water in the form of a large expanse (LAKE); others, water as running in a large body or in a small body (RIVER and BROOK); still other terms express water in the form of RAIN, DEW, WAVE, and FOAM. It is perfectly conceivable that this variety of ideas, each of which is expressed by a single independent term in English, might be expressed in other languages by derivations from the same term.

Another example of the same kind, the words for SNOW in Eskimo, may be given. Here we find one word, *aput*, expressing SNOW ON THE GROUND; another one, *qana*, FALLING SNOW; a third one, *piqsirpoq*, DRIFTING SNOW; and a fourth one, *qimuqsuq*, A SNOWDRIFT. (Boas, 1911, pp. 145–146)

large number of "Eskimo words for snow". Martin traces how Boas used the example to illustrate a way one language might use unrelated terms to express a concept for which another language might use phrasal modifications of one term; Boas cited four different root forms in Eskimo that in English are expressed by modifications of one term (*snow*). Boas also gave examples where distinct words of English correspond to phrasal modifications of the same word in another language: in Dakota, *xtaka* TO GRIP is used with modifiers to express various kinds of gripping for which English has distinct words. However, this simple and well-known linguistic idea – that different languages lexicalize different concepts – gradually morphed, in both the popular and academic publications, into an urban legend about the Eskimos having X different words for snow, for ever-increasing values of X.

Geoff Pullum, in a quarterly opinion feature published in the technical journal *Natural Language and Linguistic Theory* over several years, wrote a humorous column (Pullum, 1989) intending to draw linguists' attention to Martin's article. Pullum's article was later republished as a chapter in a book that reprinted these essays, and had this particular article's title ("The Great Eskimo Vocabulary Hoax") as a part of the book's title (Pullum, 1991). One of the earliest uses of Boas's example was in Whorf (1940b; p. 216 in Carroll, 1956b; p. 277 in Carroll et al., 2012), who did not mention any number at all but rather cited five English phrases denoting snow types and said that "To an Eskimo, this all-inclusive word [English *snow*] would be almost unthinkable". From there further commentators allowed the number to become larger and larger. Pullum's examples run to 200.

We also remark at this stage (before returning to the more general topic) that the alleged Whorfian implications about worldview are not, for Boas or Whorf, to be found in the lexicon but rather are to be found in *abstract patterns* that members of word-classes share. So, for these theorists, issues about "how many words does the language have for phenomenon X" is not really germane to the linguistic relativity issue discussed by Whorf and colleagues. That is, these implications reside in linguistic structure rather than the lexicon; and in word forms only as a consequence of these patterns. See the discussion in §3.5 below.

(A yet further example of this is cited for SEAL, where Boas finds different words for seals "in different conditions".) Other examples Boas gives illustrate the reverse, with English having multiple words for what are modifications of a single basic form in another language:

> As an example of the manner in which terms that we express by independent words are grouped under one concept, the Dakota language may be selected. The terms *naxta'ka* TO KICK, *paxta'ka* TO BIND IN BUNDLES, *yaxta'ka* TO BITE, *ic'a'xtaka* TO BE NEAR TO, *boxta'ka* TO POUND, are all derived from the common element *xtaka* TO GRIP, which holds them together, while we use distinct words for expressing the various ideas.
>
> Thus it happens that each language, from the point of view of another language, may be arbitrary in its classifications; that what appears as a single simple idea in one language may be characterized by a series of distinct word-stems in another. (Boas, 1911, p. 146–147)

Although much of the foregoing has suggested (to some) a support for a form of what is considered to be linguistic relativity, it seems pretty clear that Boas himself did not wish to draw this sort of conclusion from the simple observation of the possibilities of different languages using different strategies (distinct lexical items vs. derivations from a common base item) of word formation.[21] Other remarks of Boas show a much more muted acceptance of such an implication:

> It seems very questionable in how far the restriction of the use of certain grammatical forms can really be conceived as a hindrance in the formulation of generalized ideas. It seems much more likely that the lack of these forms is due to the lack of their need. (Boas, 1911, p. 149)
>
> Thus it would seem that the obstacles to generalized thought inherent in the form of a language are of minor importance only, and that presumably the language alone would not prevent a people from advancing to more generalized forms of thinking if the general

---

[21] And Whorf himself was not interested – at least not primarily – in different word-forms like these. He was more interested in "hidden, unconscious features" of one's language. See the discussion of "cryptotypes" in §3.5 below.

state of their culture should require expression of such thought; that under these conditions, the language would be moulded rather by the cultural state. It does not seem likely, therefore, that there is any direct relation between the culture of a tribe and the language they speak, except in so far as the form of the language will be moulded by the state of culture, but not in so far as a certain state of culture is conditioned by morphological traits of the language.

Thus we have found that language does not furnish the much-looked-for means of discovering differences in the mental status of different races. (Boas, 1911, p. 154)

In conclusion here, it seems that—although Boas had an incredible range of information about the wide divergencies between SAE languages and American Indian languages (and the divergencies among these American Indian languages), and also much knowledge of many of their cultures—he did not draw any distinctly linguistic relativity conclusions concerning the relationships holding between their languages and their cultures. On the other hand, his weak denials (as just cited here) perhaps leave the door ajar for others to open more completely. And we shall explore whether and how Sapir and Whorf might have done so.

2.4 A Miscellany of Reactions to Linguistic Relativity, Independent of Sapir and Whorf (1875–1949)

The lineage of Whorfianism we've been tracing (Herder ↦ Humboldt ↦ Boas ↦ Sapir ↦ Whorf) is of course highly simplified and overly idealized. For there were others—some preceding or contemporary with Herder, others influenced in one way or another by von Humboldt—who were in some way influenced (either positively or negatively) by this simple lineage. In this section we give a handful of quotations from philosophers, linguists, and anthropologists who reacted either favourably or unfavourably to what we've called linguistic relativity, but prior to or independently of Whorf's popular works.

Note that other writers from the previous century might also be cited, some showing a closer affinity with Humboldt, and some suggesting the Boasian view concerning the equality of all "cultures".[22]

> Every single language has. . . . its own peculiar framework of established distinctions, its shapes and forms of thought, into which, for the human being who learns that language as his "mother-tongue", is cast the content and product of his mind, his store of impressions, however acquired, his experience and knowledge of the world. This is what is sometimes called the "inner form" of language, the shape and cast of thought as fitted to a certain body of expression. But it comes as the result of external influence; it is an accompaniment of the process by which the individual acquires the body of expression itself. . . . It amounts simply to this: that the mind which was capable of doing otherwise has been led to view things in this particular way, to group them in a certain manner, to contemplate them consciously in these and those relations. (Whitney, 1875, pp. 21–22 [cited in Koerner, 1992, pp. 174–175; Lee, 1996, p. 90; Allan, 2010, p. 238])

> So then you see that it is the thought of past humanity imbedded in our language which makes Nature to be what she is for us; and the world in which we live is a world of general conceptions, and these are determined by language and expressed by signs. If the way in which these general conceptions are bound by previous thought of society, it follows that our ancestors have made the world to be what it is for us". (Clifford, 1880, pp. 110–111)

> The words in which we think are channels of thought which we have not dug ourselves, but which we found ready-made for us. . . . Language . . . is not outside the mind, but *is* the outside of the mind. Language is very thought as much as thought is very language. (Müller, 1887, p. 210–211)

---

[22] But in the following discussion, we just cite Max Müller (1862–1919), the German-American Egyptologist; William Whitney (1827–1894), possibly the best known American linguist of the century; and William Kingdon Clifford (1845–1879), the widely admired English mathematician-philosopher-logician.

SOME HISTORICAL ANTECEDENTS 27

These quotations all seem to provide some support – however muted – for linguistic relativity. Bertrand Russell, the well-known logician-philosopher, expressed a worry that was also a concern of the logical positivists: that there is a mismatch between natural language and "reality". It's usually thought not to be clear how we could know the "true form of reality" directly – apart from how our language described it – so that we could see exactly how natural language is misleading us. But looking at the differences manifested by different languages, we can know that there must be *some* sort of "mis-calibration". Be that as it may, this is again a type of "support" for the existence of linguistic relativity, only now seeing it as harmful rather than some sort of feature merely to be acknowledged.[23]

> The subject-predicate logic, with the substance-attribute metaphysic, are a case in point. it is doubtful whether either would have been invented by people speaking a non-Aryan language; certainly they do not seem to have arisen in China, except in connection with Buddhism, which brought Indian philosophy with it. . . .] In these respects language misleads us both by its vocabulary and by its syntax. We must be on our guard in both respects if our logic is not to lead to a false metaphysic. (Russell, 1924, p. 367)

The notion of different communities having different worldviews was also a feature of various mid-twentieth-century Continental (especially German) linguists, anthropologists, and philosophers, as a number of commentators have noted. For example, in an article appearing in Hoijer (1954a, a work we will discuss hereafter), Greenberg (1954, pp. 3–4), mentioned that the "German view" of Herder and von Humboldt had also found a place in the (then recent) Continental philosophical(-ish) literature – naming Ernst Cassirer (1933), Jost Trier (1932), Leo Weisgerber (1949; 1950), and Claude Lévi-Strauss (1951). Cassirer and Weisgerber were strong exponents of von Humboldt's view, said Greenberg, citing them as follows:

---

[23] Compare this quote from Russell with the similar one in §3.4 here from Whorf.

the difference between languages derives, in his [von Humboldt's] view, less from differences in sounds and signs than from differences of world-view. (Cassirer, 1933, p. 20)

As an intermediate psychic realm, [language] is clearly distinct from the area of 'objective meanings,' particularly in the sense that it is not a simple reflection of the world of objects, but rather embodies the result of an intellectual remolding of this world. (Weisgerber, 1949, p. 13)

Despite these few scholars who apparently agreed with at least a part of linguistic relativity, we can also see that, prior to Sapir and Whorf, the idea of linguistic relativity was not very widely accepted or even acknowledged – this despite the fact that the claims of Herder (and "his group" of anti-Kantians) and von Humboldt that we've reviewed in this chapter seem to hold to at least a portion of Whorfianism. Rather, it seems that most of the thinkers who bothered about non-European languages thought (contra Boas) that the purpose or intent of a language was to reflect "the true reality", and that differences among language-groups were really just a matter of one culture being more "primitive" than another – or perhaps (as a holdover of the earlier European thought) that these peoples were in some way inherently inferior to European peoples and that was borne out in their language. (Boas and all his students were adamantly opposed to these views, but it was still apparently the opinion of a number of scholars, as well as "the ordinary (European and American) citizen".)

3
Edward Sapir and Benjamin Lee Whorf: Lives, Research, and Whorfianism

3.1 The Life of Sapir (1884–1939)

This section is about the life of Sapir, and not (except incidentally) about his works that concern linguistic relativity. Discussion of his thoughts on topics of language, culture, worldview, relativity, and so forth is in §3.2.

History (and the ethnolinguistic academic tradition) seems to have determined that Edward Sapir was Boas's premier student in the area of ethnolinguistic studies. Sapir is known for both the quality and the quantity of his empirical research on specific languages and for the breadth and clarity of his theoretical vision. He also played an important role in developing the subfield of culture and personality, which is concerned with the interaction between psychological functioning and cultural patterns. His concern for the relationship between language and thought stands at the intersection of these two areas of interest.

However, Sapir was, by far, not the only eminent anthropologist Boas mentored. Among the others were Alfred L. Kroeber, Boas's first PhD student (1901). Kroeber, along with another Boas student, Robert Lowie, started the anthropology program at the University of California, Berkeley. Others were Fay-Cooper Cole (who started the anthropology program at University of Chicago), Alexander Goldenweiser (who started the anthropology program at the New School for Social Research), Leslie Spier (who started the anthropology program at the University of Washington), and Melville Herskovits (who started the anthropology program at Northwestern University), as well as Ruth Benedict, Ruth Bunzel, Jules Henry, George Herzog, Adamson Hoebel, Margaret Mead, Ashley Montagu, Paul Radin, and Gene Weltfish. Many of these scholars were editors of the American Anthropological Association journal, *American Anthropologist*, as were their students, some time later. Boas and his students were also an influence on various philosophers and "cultural intellectuals," such as Claude Lévi-Strauss, who interacted with Boas and the Boasians during his stay in New York in the 1940s.

We have already mentioned that Sapir's MA thesis of 1905 (published as Sapir, 1907) was an exposition and critique of Herder's 1772 Berlin Academy Prize-winning essay *Treatise on the Origin of Language*. But even though Herder did discuss (albeit in an a priori way) the issues of culture and worldview, and their impact on language, Sapir's own writings did not, until later in his academic career, put forward thoughts that we would now consider to be aligned with linguistic relativity.

Darnell (1990) records the life of Sapir, focussing especially on his work with numerous Amerindian languages. In the summer of 1906 Sapir collected data on Takelma, and this work became his doctoral dissertation of 1908, under Boas. It foreshadowed his later formulation of the concept of a phoneme by introducing the notion of "pseudo-sounds". Before the completion of his dissertation, Sapir had spent a year (1907–1908) at the University of California, Berkeley, at the invitation of Kroeber, with funding from a grant Kroeber had (to rapidly produce a survey of California languages and cultures).[1] According to Regna Darnell, however, Sapir's "insistence on carefully working out the details of the investigation" of the nearly extinct language Yana, which was an important part of Kroeber's grant, made Sapir egregiously late for the demands of the grant, and so Kroeber had to release him. Darnell (1990, p. 28) remarks, "unsurprisingly, Sapir was unable to write up his Yana material during the year of his appointment. Kroeber's correspondence with Sapir over the ensuing decade was interspersed with pleas for a completed manuscript. Sapir, who

---

[1] A priority of the then-California government, in the face of the disappearance of tribal cultures.

still felt that he would have finished Yana if he had been given funding to stay at the University of California, procrastinated over this commitment more than any other." In 1919 Kroeber found funding so that Sapir could return to California to work on the Yana language again. But as Darnell (1990, p. 29) remarks, "the problem [of producing a Yana grammar] was only compounded by Sapir's summer working... on a different dialect of Yana – which Sapir also failed to work up for publication. Kroeber legitimately felt that Sapir had twice failed to meet his commitments".

After his unsuccessful stay at the University of California in 1907-1908, when it became clear that he wouldn't be appointed to replace Pliny Goddard (who had resigned effective in 1909), Sapir provisionally accepted George Gordan's offer of the Harrison fellowship at the University of Pennsylvania, to begin in October 1909. Sapir left California early to return to New York in order to defend his dissertation. During his time at the University of Pennsylvania, he did "field work" (much of it in the city of Philadelphia with a native speaker of Southern Paiute), culminating in the development of Sapir's notion of a phoneme in later years). His research into this language led him to formulate the idea that a phoneme was not just a theoretical linguistic abstraction, but was a psychologically real feature of the human language system. The Southern Paiute grammar was intended for Boas's *Handbook of American Indian Languages*, and Boas urged him to complete a preliminary version while funding for the publication remained available, but Sapir did not want to compromise on quality, and in the end the *Handbook* had to go to press without Sapir's piece. Other factors also interfered: Boas's forced retirement (due to "an ill-considered public accusation of inappropriate wartime actions by practicing anthropologists" Darnell, 1990, p. 37);[2] issues involving the

---

[2] Although Darnell doesn't discuss the details of this episode, Wikipedia (https://en.wikipedia.org/wiki/Franz_Boas#Scientist_as_activist) reports that in 1919 Boas discovered that four anthropologists, led by Sylvanus Morley, were spying for the US government while conducting research in Mexico. They were looking for evidence of German submarine bases and collected intelligence on Mexican political figures. Boas was outraged by this and published an angry letter in the *Nation* denouncing them and accusing them of prostituting science in an unpardonable way and forfeiting the right to be classed as scientists. The American Anthropological Association and the National Research Council passed a resolution censuring Boas.

American Anthropological Association's phonetics committee; and various other factors. (Again, see Darnell, 1990, pp. 34–38).

Sapir's perceived slowness in publication convinced him, according to Darnell, that he would never get a permanent position at a US research institution. And thus he accepted a position at the Canadian Geological Survey, which wanted him to form a federal institute of anthropology in Canada. He spent the years 1910–1925 in Canada, travelling to various places in Canada – some quite remote (he started at the very beginning of the position with fieldwork on the Nootka of Vancouver Island) – to document the native languages. He also became an advocate for the rights of the Indigenous Peoples, including, famously, fighting for a retraction of the Canadian law that outlawed potlatches by the tribes of the West Coast. During his time in Canada, Sapir published two very influential works: *Time Perspective in the Aboriginal American Culture* of 1916 and the very famous *Language* of 1921. He also coauthored a report advocating a standardization of the orthography for Indigenous language transcriptions.

After some considerable familial misfortunes, Sapir was eager to return to the United States. Darnell, 1990, pp. 202–237) describes the numerous issues that were involved in Sapir receiving an offer from the University of Chicago, which he accepted in 1925. According to Darnell, Sapir thrived in the wide range of intellectually stimulating activities he participated in there. These included radio debates, the popular courses he taught on psychology, his participation in poetry and music clubs, the (wealthy) Chicago Jewish community, and a cadre of new friends in various different disciplines at the university. But most of all, his new life with a new wife.

James Angell, president of Yale University in 1931, was an outsider who was the first president of Yale who was not also a graduate of Yale. He wanted Yale to become a more visible academic center and viewed Sapir as the type of "star" who could make inroads into the monies of the Rockefeller social science funding. To lure Sapir to Yale, Angell appointed Sapir as the Sterling Professor, promising him that he would head a new department of cultural anthropology (previously subsumed within Sociology), with several new appointments, ties to the Peabody Museum in New Haven and the Bishop Museum in Honolulu, funding for fieldwork in America and abroad, and a new

Division of Human Geography made up of faculty from throughout the social sciences. However, as Darnell reports (1990, p. 400), Sapir's friend, Robert Hutchins, president of the University of Chicago and former Yale dean of law ... warned Sapir: "Look, we can't match Yale's prestige, nor salary, nor liberal research budgets, but be warned that you are going into a far narrower society and intellectual tradition and will meet strong anti-Semitism.... Sapir ignored the warning."

Sapir's time at Yale heralded a new beginning for American anthropology, but there was considerable infighting and in the end, the "Camelot" Sapir might have envisioned never came about. The depressing details are recounted in Darnell (1998), based on her examination of departmental and interdepartmental minutes and letters in the archives of Yale University, as well as the reminiscences of some of the then-still-living members of this episode in the history of academia. Darnell also remarks (1998, p. 400–401) that Sapir never thrived at Yale, where – as one of only four Jewish faculty members out of 569 – he was denied membership to the Graduate Club, where the senior faculty regularly met to discuss academic business.[3] And (apparently) Jews were not permitted to teach undergraduates. He also missed the vibrant intellectual scene of the city of Chicago ... something that New Haven did not possess.

Despite all this – and despite his continual intellectual (and territorial) disputes with many of the established faculty members – Sapir managed a robust group of graduate students in anthropological linguistics, as well as some postdoctoral scholars.[4] This group included many of the linguists (and anthropological linguists) who formed the center of American linguistics in the 1930–1960 era, including Mary Haas, Morris Swadish, Harry Hoijer, Charles Hockett, David Mandelbaum, Carl Voegelin, Stanley Newman, Feng-ui Li, Gerge Herzog ... and of course, Benjamin Lee Whorf.

---

[3] Darnell remarks that "oral tradition" says the denial was to the Faculty Club, but that is not correct. Sapir was (eventually) admitted to the Faculty Club – the only Jewish member. She also remarks that it "was unheard of that a Sterling Professor could be blackballed" from the Graduate Club and speculates on possible reasons that were not directly aimed at Sapir personally.

[4] In discussing this, Darnell (1990, p. 366) remarks that the term 'student' is to be used "very broadly, to include almost everyone he [Sapir] had contact with, and not only the few formal students he trained. Certainly, both anthropologists and linguists considered themselves Sapir's students on the basis of quite minimal exposure."

In the summer of 1937, Sapir taught at the Linguistic Institute of the Linguistic Society of America in Ann Arbor. And he started having more serious problems with a heart condition that had initially been diagnosed a couple of years earlier. He was due for a sabbatical leave in 1937–1938, and he had intended to go to China, but the Japan-China War had made this unfeasible. So Sapir instead arranged to spend the year teaching in Hawaii – as Yale University was affiliated with the Bishop Museum in Honolulu, and Sapir was friends with some of the Honolulu staff. But the heart attack that summer of 1937 required him to postpone going to Hawaii until the second semester; and then, as his health problems unfolded during the first term, it was determined that he had to spend the entire academic year in New York for medical treatment. Further heart problems led to his resigning his chair, although he kept teaching (but with a reduced course load).

In preparation for the sabbatical, arrangements were made to cover Sapir's courses: Swadish taught "Primitive Languages", Trager taught "Phonetics", and Whorf was appointed "Lecturer in Anthropology" and taught "American Indian Linguistics".[5] (We discuss Whorf's appointment as a lecturer and discuss how he came to be appointed in §3.6.1.) And G. P. Murdock, who had been at Yale since 1928 as "the anthropologist among the sociologists", advised some of Sapir's students. After Sapir's death in 1939, Murdock became the chair of the Anthropology Department. Murdock, who according to Darnell (1990, pp. 346ff and 416–417), Murdock despised the Boasian paradigm of cultural anthropology and dismantled most of Sapir's efforts to integrate anthropology, psychology, and linguistics Murdock thus became the executioner of Sapir's "Yale Camelot", as discussed in Darnell (1998).

3.2 Sapir's Linguistic Relativity

We should point out that most of Sapir's writings do not mention – in either a positive or negative way – anything like what we would characterize as relativism about language and culture, and instead

---

[5] Darnell (1990) also remarks that during this time Whorf also wrote drafts of many of his later works, as well as conducting his fire-prevention work.

are straightforward descriptions of a wide variety of American Indian languages. Nonetheless, there are various places where his words are naturally understood as being either pro- or anti-Whorfian. And we here gather some of them.

In setting forth Sapir's relevant views on linguistic relativity here, we let Sapir himself mostly do the explanation of his views – sometimes with a little of the background information concerning these sayings. Sapir himself seems to have moved from an early "anti-Sapir/Whorf" point of view to his later and better-known Whorfianism. His very famous *Language* (1921) contains many of these earlier antirelativistic statements, for example as announced in the table of contents, where he describes his second-to-last chapter (Chapter 10: "Language, Race and Culture") this way: "Naïve tendency to consider linguistic, racial, and cultural groupings as congruent. Race and language need not correspond. Cultural and linguistic boundaries not identical. Coincidences between linguistic cleavages and those of language and culture due to historical, not intrinsic psychological, causes. Language does not in any deep sense "reflect" culture" (Sapir, 1921, p. ix).

In this chapter, Sapir makes an extended argument against the view that there is any particular connection to be found between and among the three areas mentioned in the title (language, race, culture). Apparently the popular opinion of the time also included a notion of "racial or national temperament" (Sapir, 1921, pp. 216). After he concludes that "there is no profound causal relation between the development of language and the specific development of race and of culture", he refers to this popular opinion concerning "temperament", imagining this rejoinder from a believer: "but surely . . . there must be some relation between language and culture, and between language and at least that intangible aspect of race that we call "temperament." Is it not inconceivable that the particular collective qualities of mind that have fashioned a culture are not precisely the same as were responsible for the growth of a particular linguistic morphology?" (p. 216).

Sapir answers this popular opinion, saying (among other also relevant things):

> even granted that temperament has a certain value for the shaping of culture, difficult though it may be to say just how, it does not follow that it has the same value for the shaping of language. It is impossible

to show that the form of a language has the slightest connection with national temperament. . . . I am convinced that it is futile to look in linguistic structure for differences corresponding to the temperamental variations which are supposed to be correlated with race. . . . Nor can I believe that culture and language are in any true sense causally related. Culture may be defined as *what* a society does and thinks. Language is a particular *how* of thought. It is difficult to see what particular causal relations may be expected to subsist between a selected inventory of experience (culture, a significant selection made by society) and the particular manner in which the society expresses all experience. (Sapir, 1921, pp. 217)

But a few years later we find him writing in what we might think is a more "extreme" form of Whorfianism than is to be found explicitly in Whorf himself. (We follow up on this difference where we discuss Whorf's own remarks in §3.4.)

Sapir's earlier attitude seems to have rather suddenly changed within a few years, and towards the end of a popular article (Sapir, 1924) we find him introducing the term *relativity* in conjunction with *concepts* and *form of thought* for what we think is the first time in his discussions of how language works and how linguistic study can provide relevant data . . . and perhaps even in *any* discussion in the field of linguistics:

> it would be possible to go on indefinitely with such examples of incommensurable analyses of experience in different languages. The upshot of it all would be to make very real to us a kind of relativity that is generally hidden from us by our naïve acceptance of fixed habits of speech as guides to an objective understanding of the nature of experience. This is the relativity of concepts or, as it might be called, the relativity of the form of thought. . . . For its understanding, the comparative data of linguistics are a *sine qua non*. It is the appreciation of the relativity of the form of thought which results from linguistic study that is perhaps the most liberalizing thing about it. What fetters the mind and benumbs the spirit is ever the dogged acceptance of absolutes. (Sapir, 1924, p. 155)

And in his contribution to a symposium in 1927 devoted to "The Unconscious" (the symposium had a mandate to "learn consciously to utilize the integrative action of the unconscious"), Sapir waxed enthusiastically about the patterns that can be gleaned from a study of languages used by cultures that are far distant from one's own.[6] His idea was that the use of at least certain areas of language carried out by individuals in their social interactions manifested a type of unconscious mental functioning. To bolster this, he pointed to verbal interactions in social groups, saying:

> language is not merely a more or less systematic inventory of the various items of experience which seem relevant to the individual, as is so often naïvely assumed, but is also a self-contained, creative symbolic organization which not only refers to experience largely acquired without its help but actually defines experience for us by reason of its formal completeness and because of our unconscious projection of its implicit expectations into the field of experience.... Such categories as number, gender, case, tense, mode, voice, "aspect"... are, of course, derivative of experience at last analysis, but, once abstracted from experience, they are systematically elaborated in language and are not so much discovered in experience as imposed upon it because of the tyrannical hold that linguistic form has upon our orientation in the world. (Sapir, 1927a, p. 578)

Perhaps Sapir's best-known statement concerning and endorsing Whorfianism is the following lengthy one. Like the quotation just given, this one seems to promote a stronger or more far-reaching type of linguistic relativity than we find in Whorf.

> Language is a guide to 'social reality'. Though language is not ordinarily thought of as of essential interest to the students of social science, it powerfully conditions all our thinking about social problems and processes. Human beings do not live in the objective world

---

[6] Lee (1996, p. 34) says of this article: "Sapir's brilliant article of 1927 ... will perhaps never be equalled for the lucidity and succinctness with which the complexity and subtlety of socially patterned behaviors of all kinds are introduced and explained."

alone, nor alone in the world of social activity as ordinarily understood, but are very much at the mercy of the particular language which has become the medium of expression for their society. It is quite an illusion to imagine that one adjusts to reality essentially without the use of language and that language is merely an incidental means of solving specific problems of communication or reflection. The fact of the matter is that the 'real world' is to a large extent unconsciously built up on the language habits of the group. No two languages are ever sufficiently similar to be considered as representing the same social reality. The worlds in which different societies live are distinct worlds, not merely the same world with different labels attached. . . . Even comparatively simple acts of perception are very much more at the mercy of the social patterns called words than we might suppose. If one draws some dozen lines, for instance, of different shapes, one perceives them as divisible into such categories as 'straight', 'crooked', 'curved', 'zigzag' because of the classificatory suggestiveness of the linguistic terms themselves. We see and hear and otherwise experience very largely as we do because the language habits of our community predispose certain choices of interpretation. (Sapir, 1929, pp. 209-210)

The foregoing passages were written before Sapir and Whorf had any interaction with one another.[7] The force of these claims of relativity seems to be quite a bit stronger and more pointed than what we hear from Whorf in §3.4.

Although Sapir (as well as other anthropologists) had emphasized that the language of the non-SAE communities that anthropologists were studying departed radically from the SAE languages, and that there was a major difference in the speakers' worldviews, it was apparently not a topic for them to try to determine which way the influence went: Did the worldview arise initially and hence language adapted to reinforce it? Or was it the other way around? Perhaps a language for ordinary life – subsisting, mating, and so on – became more and

---

[7] As we point out in §3.3, Whorf and Sapir were first introduced to one another in 1928, at a conference, but no lengthy or private meeting took place until late 1930, according to Darnell (1990, pp. 375-382) and Lee (1996, p. 10).

more sophisticated, embodying what one might call a "special viewpoint" from which to describe time, the stars, fire, life, and the place of humans in the universe generally. Perhaps the language even changed so as to better enunciate the ways invisible forces kept the universe "at peace with itself", and so forth. In short, the language generated a worldview (which may be different from "culture").[8]

3.3 The Life of Whorf (1897–1941)

This section is about the life of Whorf, and not (except incidentally) about his works that concern linguistic relativity. Discussion of his thoughts on topics of language, culture, worldview, relativity, and so forth are in sections §3.4 and §3.5.

Highlights of the life of Whorf are recounted Carroll's introduction to *Language, Thought & Reality* (Carroll, 1956a, 2012). Further details can be gleaned from Lee (1996) and Darnell (1990), among others, including the very interesting (if idiosyncratic) Edwards (2017). Whorf graduated from MIT in 1918 with a BSc in chemical engineering and began his lifelong career with the Hartford Fire Insurance Company. He apparently was an extremely able fire-prevention engineer, and rose quickly within the company. The company approved his various trips to Mexico and the southwestern US, as well as his later attendance at Yale to further his linguistics education with Sapir. Carroll says (1956a, p. 5; 2012, p. 6): "it may have been that the company was proud of his accomplishments in linguistics and anthropology, and we know that it was liberal in granting him occasional leaves to carry on these activities." Whatever the background reasons the Hartford Fire Insurance Company might have had for granting Whorf such latitude in arranging his work schedules to accommodate his academic endeavours, they must not have taken away from his work schedule, since the company continually promoted Whorf to higher

---

[8] The quandary posed here – that perhaps worldview directs language development, which in turn is reflected in the culture of those users, and that this in turn directs one's worldview – was already noted in the early discussions of Whorfianism, and was called "the chicken and egg" puzzle by Greenberg (1954, p. 9), although he also applied the phrase to more specific cases where he *did* think an ordering *could* be inferred.

positions (e.g., special agent, 1928), until at the time of his early death (1941) he held there the fairly high (and elected) position of assistant secretary. He also made time for community activities such as serving on the fire prevention committee of the Hartford Chamber of Commerce, and giving public lectures to historical societies, men's clubs, libraries, and so on.

Whorf seems to have also had an early interest in a presumed conflict between science and (Christian) religion, and he spent some early years teaching himself ancient Hebrew and expanded this to include Sanskrit. There has been some thought that Whorf found "mystical properties" in language and that this induced him to study the "esoteric philosopher" Antoine Fabre d'Oliver, where Whorf found thoughts about "the symbolic function of grammar." (See Carroll, 1956b, pp. 7-13; Carroll et al., 2012, pp. 8-13; Lee, 1996, pp. 1.) The idea seems to be that each letter (of ancient Hebrew, anyway) somehow has a common meaning wherever it occurs, but of course such a meaning would have to be very "abstract", and would have to be teased out from a study of all its occurrences. According to Carroll and Lee, this was the origin of Whorf's much later idea of "cryptotypes". In 1926, Whorf turned his attention to the study of Nahuatl (Aztec), and "around 1928" to Mayan hieroglyphs,[9] using materials he found in the Hartford Public Library. He corresponded with some Mexican archaeology and linguistics scholars, and worked on translating a page of an old Mexican manuscript of which the library had a photo. He read a paper on this at the Twenty-third International Congress of Americanists in 1928 (where he first met Sapir, as part of a group) and its publication marked his first academic success. According to Carroll (1956a, p. 11; Carroll et al., 2012, p. 13), Whorf received considerable publicity for this and newspapers reported that he had "unlocked mysteries."[10] He published another Aztec translation in 1929. In 1928 he successfully applied for a Social Science Research Council fellowship, this time pursuing a theory of "oligosynthesis", or "features underlying the overt properties of the language." "He

---

[9] According to Carroll (1956a, pp. 10); Carroll et al. (2012, p. 10).

[10] However, Carroll does not cite any venues of the "considerable publicity" or names of newspapers.

argued," says Lee (1996, p. 3),"that some languages could be broken down to a very few roots or 'elements' (35 in Nahuatl) each standing 'for a certain general idea, including something of the surrounding field of related ideas into which this central idea insensibly shades off.'"[11]

In the end he used the fellowship to travel to Mexico and got access to "several excellent informants who spoke a form of Aztec which was believed to approximate ... the classical dialect of Aztec once spoken in Tenochtitlan at the time of Montezuma" (Carroll, 1956a, p. 14; 2012, p. 17). His detailed linguistic analysis was published posthumously as Whorf (1946).[12] He also

> came upon, apparently quite by chance, a band of sculptured figures which had previously escaped the close attention of scholars. His sharp observation and close familiarity with both Aztec and Maya graphic art enabled him to recognize almost immediately that these figures deviated from their usual forms as "day signs" of the Aztec calendar and showed certain resemblances to Mayan characters. This discovery of "a definite, clearly demonstrable rapport between Nahuatl hieroglyphs and early Maya ones," as Whorf regarded it, was the basis of [Whorf (1932)]. (Carroll,1956a, p. 14; 2012, pp. 17–18)

In 1931 Sapir moved to Yale, and shortly thereafter Whorf registered to take courses taught by Sapir. At around 1933, Whorf was introduced to Ernest "Eagle Plume" Naquayouma.[13] The son of a Hopi chief, Naquayouma was born (in 1906), in Second Mesa and raised in the traditional Hopi environment, although he went to the reservation school. In 1923 he joined a troop of "show Indians" touring the

---

[11] Lee cites an unpublished work by Whorf from 1928: "Notes on the oligosynthetic comparison of Nahuatl and Piman, with special reference to Tepecano".

[12] Whorf also had various other articles published in this volume, notably "The Hopi Language, Toreva Dialect" and "Chiricahua Apache".

[13] Carroll suggests it was "probably" Sapir who introduced the two; but Robert Edwards (2017, p. 26) suggests it was "likely through [Helen Clifton] Roberts". (Roberts and Naquayouma had a standing relationship to record songs of Hopi sung by Naquayouma, as we mention shortly.) Regna Darnell (1990, p. 377) is noncommital, remarking only that Whorf sought funding (for Naquayouma as his informant) from Elsie Clews Parsons, a patron of ethnographic work on southwestern Amerindian languages and culture. (The letters cited by Darnell make it seem that the request was made in 1933.)

country, dancing at shows and selling crafts. During the late 1920s Naquayouma started recording Hopi songs with ethnomusicologist Helen Clifton Roberts (see Edwards, 2017, p. 26). Around 1932 he moved to Brooklyn with his wife and children, in order to find work. In order to earn money, Naquayouma met with Whorf often – usually in New York, but sometimes Whorf paid for a train ticket for Naquayouma to travel to Hartford. Despite the fact of having been hired for pay, the existing letters (all from Naquayouma) suggest a real friendship. Naquayouma was Whorf's key source of data about the Hopi language and served as the deciding editor of Alexander Stephen's Hopi-English glossary. (Stephen had recently died and Boas was to publish Stephen's 1936 *Hopi Journal*. Boas asked the Hopi ethnographer Elsie Parsons to edit the book and asked Whorf to review and correct the glossary. Hoijer sent Whorf the only other existing Hopi glossary, which had been compiled by Mennonite missionaries. On comparing Stephen's glossary with the Mennonite one, plus his own notes from his work with Naquayouma, Whorf told Boas that Stephen's work was so full of errors that it was worthless. Whorf successfully recommended to Boas that he [Boas] hire Naquayouma to edit the glossary.)

During the 1930s, Whorf was simultaneously studying with Sapir and working as a fire-prevention engineer, as well as publishing many papers and working on books he would never finish. During this time he also visited the Second Mesa to confirm the information Naquayouma had given him about the Hopi language.

Whorf died in July 1941 at the age of 44. Carroll(1956a, p. 21; 2012, p. 27) says it was "after a long and lingering illness, during which he valiantly struggled to keep up his study and his writing." Although it is not clear from Carroll's introduction just how long Whorf had been ill, we might note that between 1938 and his death he published three journal articles (in *Language; Studies in Linguistics*; and the *International Journal of American Linguistics*), the Whorf's Sapir Memorial Paper, four papers in edited anthologies, the three papers in MIT's *Technology Review*, a book review in *American Anthropologist*, the paper for the*Theosophist*, 14 short entries in the journal *Main Currents in Modern Thought*, and an article on fire prevention.[14]

---

[14] See the Bibliography for full details of this work, Whorf 1941

3.4 Whorf on Linguistic Relativity

As we did with Sapir, in this section we present Whorf's thoughts on what linguistic relativism is through the various statements he gave about it. We postpone until §3.5 discussing his views on the specific types of evidence he thought were relevant. An important aspect of Whorf's rationales for his relativism is the notion of a *cryptotype*, but we will not come to explaining that until after we first cite some of his pronouncements about relativism. (The material on cryptotypes is in §3.5.) After that, in §3.6, we discuss some of the disputes and reactions to those pieces of evidence. We introduce what has been called the "scientific interpretation" of linguistic relativity and the search for "scientific evidence" later, in §4.

Although it is clear even in Whorf's early writings that he was favourably disposed towards some views about language that might be called "relativistic", it is mostly his contribution to the Sapir Memorial Conference (Whorf, 1941b), his article for the Theosophical journal the *Theosophist* (Whorf, 1942), and his three rather popular works written late in his life for the MIT publication *Technology Review* (Whorf, 1940a, b, 1941a), that are regularly cited in discussions about Whorfianism.[15]

> We are thus introduced to a *new principle of relativity*, which holds that all observers are not led by the same physical evidence to the same picture of the universe[16], unless their linguistic backgrounds are similar, or can in some way be calibrated.... The *relativity of all conceptual systems*, ours included, and their dependence upon language stand revealed. (Whorf, 1940b; p. 214 in Carroll, 1956b; p. 274 in Carroll et al., 2012)

> We dissect nature along lines laid down by our native languages. The categories and types that we isolate from the world of phenomena we do not find there because they stare every observer in the face; on the contrary, the world is presented in a kaleidoscopic flux of

---
[15] However, we should also keep in mind Carroll's remark that "these latter papers were grounded upon a solid foundation of linguistic analysis done much ". Carroll (1956a, p. 18; 2012, p. 22).

[16] Presumably, Whorf means "... holds that not all observers are led by the same physical evidence to the same picture...".

impressions which has to be organized by our minds— – and this means largely by the linguistic systems in our minds. We cut nature up, organize it into concepts, and ascribe significances as we do, largely because we are parties to an agreement to organize it in this way – an agreement that holds throughout our speech community and is codified in the patterns of our language. (Whorf, 1940b; p. 213 in Carroll, 1956b; p. 272 in Carroll et al., 2012)

... no individual is free to describe nature with absolute impartiality but is constrained to certain modes of interpretation even while he thinks himself most free. (Whorf, 1940b; p. 214 in Carroll, 1956b; p. 274 in Carroll et al., 2012)

... users of markedly different grammars are pointed by their grammars toward different types of observations and different evaluations of externally similar acts of observation, and hence are not equivalent as observers but must arrive at somewhat different views of the world. (Whorf, 1940a; p. 221 in Carroll, 1956b; pp. 282–283 in Carroll et al., 2012)

... facts are unlike to speakers whose language background provides for unlike formulation of them. (Whorf, 1941a; p. 235 in Carroll, 1956b; p. 301 in Carroll et al., 2012)

The final quotation that we offer from Whorf seems quite similar to the one we cited from Bertrand Russell in §2.4, although so far as we know, Whorf never remarked about having read any of Russell's works.

Science . . . has not yet freed itself from the illusory necessities of common logic which are only at bottom necessities of grammatical pattern in Western Aryan grammar; [e.g.,] necessities for substances which are only necessities for substantives in certain sentence positions... (Whorf, 1942; pp. 269–270 in Carroll (1956b); p. 344 in Carroll et al. (2012)

These are all the standardly cited remarks that Whorf made concerning Whorfianism in his published works. (That said, there are many more remarks throughout Whorf's writings that bolster or suggest his support for linguistic relativity, especially in the later works and some of his unpublished work. Some comments of that type also occur in his citations of "evidence" for Whorfian claims, as we will show in the next section.) For Whorf these citations seem to be simultaneously "working hypotheses" and conclusions reached from a "normal" analysis of the structure of various American Indian languages. In §3.5 and §3.6 we will look both at the sort of evidence Whorf amassed from rather a large number of these languages and, as well, at the validity or invalidity of the inferences he drew from the evidence. But we pause briefly here to compare Whorf's claims (both in this section and the next) with those of Sapir that we cited in §3.2, where we said that Sapir's claims appear to represent a stronger or more "strident" version of Whorfianism than Whorf's claims do.

In all the claims of Whorf, the relevant notion seems to be that speakers of a language *habitually* see or understand the world in a particular way. But it is apparent that he feels it possible to see/understand the world differently: indeed, he often remarks on how to do that. His informant, Naquayouma, had done it; Whorf himself claims to have done it on particular occasions about certain of the features he cites as yielding his native language's outlook on "the world". Sapir, on the other hand, seems to hold that this is not possible (or at least, his language that we cited in §3.2 seems naturally to presume that it is not possible), and his written work never presumes that he can think in the same way as one of his informants: "our language habits predispose choices of interpretation", "even simple acts of perception are at the mercy of social patterns called words", "it is an illusion to imagine that one adjusts to reality without the use of language and that language is merely an incidental means to solve specific problems of communication", "the 'real world' is unconsciously built up on the language habits of one's group", and so forth.

3.5 Whorf's (Presumed) Evidence for Relativity

In this section we look at some of the features of the Amerindian languages that Whorf used as evidence for a difference in various types of mental activity (mostly differences in "connections of concepts/ideas") that the speakers of these languages had from speakers of SAE. We start with his notion of a "cryptotype", or "covert category". As we mentioned earlier, Whorf's idea of a "hidden" feature of a language arguably had its origin in his very early thoughts occasioned by reading Fabre d'Oliver on "the symbolic function of grammar", although Whorf's develops his idea in a strongly different direction from d'Oliver's notion. Whorf's new notion was used, or alluded to, in most of his well-known later works; but it was elaborated in a more full manner only in Whorf (1945). Whorf wrote this work in 1937, in response to a request by Franz Boas for a publication in his journal, but it was found in the Boas collection only after Boas's death.

An "overt category" has some *formal mark* present in sentences containing a member of the category. The mark need not be *a part of* the member of the category (for instance, not necessarily an inflection) but could be instead a separate word or a particular patterning of the whole sentence. In English, plurality is an overt category, where the marks of plurality show up with inflection or vowel change, and sometimes only with a marking on the verb or the use of articles. A covert category is marked only in certain types of sentences and not in every sentence in which a word or element belonging to this category occurs. Membership in this class is only apparent when one tries to use it in some special types of sentence, and then it is thought that the word belongs to a class requiring some sort of special treatment. In English (according to Whorf), intransitive verbs form a covert category: they are marked by lack of the passive participle, passive voice, and causative voice. Whorf gives *go, lie, sit, rise, gleam, sleep, arrive, appear, rejoice* as verbs in this class, noting that they don't allow nouns or pronouns after the verb. Other covert categories in English are gender, where interactions with pronouns are the evidence (the "reactance") of this category.[17] (Whorf (1945) also gives a number of

---

[17] Whorf remarks that learning the gender of common names is not relevant: "I can bestow the name 'Jane' on an automobile, a skeleton, or a cannon, and it will still require

examples of "surprising" overt and covert categories in a variety of languages. An underlying idea is that cryptotypes are covert in that whatever linguistic principle or effect the cryptotype gives rise to is productive: of is manifested in terms of constraints placed on how *other* linguistic items or features can be combined (or: are prohibited from combining) with some other group of items or in some specific linguistic contexts.

It should be acknowledged that Whorf (and Sapir) did not provide evidence of the kind that would satisfy the modern ear as especially relevant to the sort of claims they made (as we cited in §3.2 and §3.4). Rather, they presented a variety of facts relevant to the languages of some group of Amerindians, remarked on how different these facts were from those in SAE languages, and concluded that the speakers of that language "must believe" such-and-so about the world and mankind's relation to it. Sometimes, more commonly in Whorf than Sapir, these pronouncements were accompanied by personal anecdotes concerning the "type of people" (peaceable, or believers in recurrence of life, recurrence of the cosmos, and the like). But these were not quantified in any way, and no particular evidence for asserting the relevant beliefs was given. As it seems now, the only evidence provided is of the form "The language manifests this-and-that set of features, very different from SAE features, and so the speakers of that language must therefore believe A, B, and C (sometimes: so they therefore will act in manners P, Q, and R)".

It must be said that the most charitable interpretation of this type of "evidence" is that the conclusions are an attempt at an *inference to the best explanation*. Sapir and Whorf seem to think that the best explanation of persons speaking in such-and-so manner is that they believed A, B, and C. And then, noting that A, B, and C are quite different from what SAE speakers believe, the observers conclude that these differences in beliefs and belief-structures are due to the features of the language.

Many of the critics of Whorfianism have objected to this train of thought on the grounds of circularity or question-begging. Others

'she' in pronominal references." Whorf (1945, p. 4), Carroll, (1956b, p. 91), Carroll et al. (2012, p. 142).

have objected to the initial inference from "speaking in such-and-so manner" to "they must believe A, B, and C". Modern attempts at verification (or disproving) these claims mostly focus on this "initial inference". (With the postscript that the A-, B-, and C-beliefs need to be manifest in some sort of observable difference from SAE speakers.)

3.6 Reactions and Disputes over the Evidence

Criticisms of linguistic relativity (and of Whorf himself) is and has been commonplace throughout the period after World War II. Of course, Whorfianism has also had its defenders during this period, but it must be said that the weight of the academic community (possibly excluding linguistic anthropology, and more recently excluding some corners of cognitive linguistics, as we will discuss in Chapter 5) has been pretty firmly against linguistic relativity. Much of the highly general argumentation seems to be between those who are enthralled by the idea that "since no one can *really* understand another, it must be impossibly more difficult to understand the speaker of another language" and those who take the stand that "we are all humans and all have the same underlying mental machinery, and therefore we are all capable of understanding one another." The latter view is buttressed by a current "universalism" in academic linguistics, as championed over the years by Noam Chomsky and in philosophy by very many (but notably by Jerry Fodor, e.g., Fodor, 1975). We discuss such topics in §5.2.

There is also a (small) group of theorists who favour Whorfianism, but nonetheless approve of some sort of universalism in this realm. These theorists like to point to the critical period[18] hypothesis concerning language acquisition. This hypothesis involves the claim that there are changes in the brain which cause the end of language's *critical period* in a child – the time after which people can no longer learn a language "as a native". These changes somehow close off the

---

[18] Not to be confused with Kant's "critical period", which refers to the period that started with his formulation of the *Critique of Pure Reason* and *The Critique of Practical Reason*. The present use refers to human linguistic development.

period during which the child language-learner is able to "truly" grasp the subtle nuances of any language other than the one(s) they were exposed to during the critical period. So these theorists favour universalism at birth and during the critical period but hold that the end of the critical period is a cause for Whorfianism after that time.[19]

The remainder of this section consists of three subsections:

(3.6.1) Some popular objections that seem to be due to misunderstandings, and a defense of Whorf's academic standing

(3.6.2) A brief recounting of the Malotki dispute with the Whorf materials on Hopi, including important underlying theoretical issues of translation

(3.6.3) General comments on translating polysynthetic languages – one's purposes will determine "correctness" of translations—and the relation of these issues to the emic-etic directions of research

3.6.1 Mis- or Non-Understandings of What Whorf Said

There is a strain of criticism against Whorfianism (in particular, and not so strongly against other linguistic relativity theories) within the academic community, and it is perhaps not easy to understand its vitriol.[20] (And perhaps also it is not so easy to understand the apparent enmity of the responses.) For instance, Steven Pinker, in his popular book *The Language Instinct*, says:

> The famous Sapir-Whorf hypothesis of linguistic determinism, stating that people's thoughts are determined by the categories

---

[19] There seems to be no agreement about when the end of the critical period occurs: some say as young as 6, others put it some time before 12, and yet others date it to puberty.

[20] Ellis (1993) says that "[the debate around Whorf's ideas] has been a strange one in which even the most prominent detractors seem to have had great difficulty in putting their finger on and formulating just what their objections were, and even in spelling out the position they were objecting to" (p. 55); "the Whorf hypothesis seems to bring out the worst in those who discuss it" (p. 57); "the nature of his original contribution does not really lie in what is commonly attacked in his work" (p. 63).

made available by their language, and its weaker version, linguistic relativity, that differences among languages cause differences in the thoughts of their speakers ... is wrong, all wrong. The idea that thought is the same as language is an example of what can be called a conventional absurdity: a statement that goes against all common sense but that everyone believes because they dimly recall having heard it somewhere. (Pinker, 1994, p. 57)

No one is really sure how Whorf came up with his outlandish claims, but his limited, badly analyzed sample of Hopi speech and his long-time leanings toward mysticism must have contributed. (Pinker, 1994, p. 63)

But the use of an established member of the Hopi nation, a native speaker of Hopi, and very many hours of detailed study of the inner workings of the Hopi language as generated by this speaker would seem to make the judgment of Steven Pinker seem out of touch with the reality of the situation.[21]

It is perhaps interesting to note a few reactions from the most established members of the field to the appearance of the formally untrained (in anthropology, ethnology, linguistics) Benjamin Whorf. When Sapir moved to Yale, Whorf immediately started auditing his courses, and soon became "just another member" of Sapir's group – those generally considered to be the premier linguistic anthropologists of the time. Before any of the famous work on linguistic relativity, we find Sapir writing in 1936 to his former student Alfred Kroeber: "Whorf is an awfully good man, largely self-made, and with a dash of genius. He is sometimes inclined to get off the central problem and indulge in marginal speculations but that merely shows the originality and adventuresome quality of his mind.... [He] is one of the most valuable

---

[21] Another academic Whorfian has reacted to these (and other) remarks of Pinker and Deutscher. Levinson 2012, pp. xi –xiii says:

That Whorf claimed "thought is the same thing as language" (Pinker, 1994, p. 57) ... is not based on a careful reading of Carroll (1956b).

Readers should thus not take either [(Pinker, 1994, p. 63)'s or (Deutscher, 2010, p. 143)'s casual dismissals of Whorf's claims to be well-founded; they will find more careful treatment in the work of [(Lee, 1991), (Lee, 1996), pp. 136–142),

... neither Pinker nor Deutscher has actually read Carroll (1956b) with any care.

American Indian linguists that we have at the present time" (quoted in Darnell, 1990, p. 375).

Leonard Bloomfield congratulated Whorf on his Uto-Aztecan work as "a splendid example of how this kind of thing ought to be done", and Alden Mason wrote to Carl Vogelin remarking that Whorf is "clearly the best man we have for the genetic problem."[22]

Darnell adds to this that "Sapir did not distinguish Whorf from other linguistic students he trained." And when Sapir was granted a sabbatical in 1937–1938 (features of which we recounted in §3.1), Leslie Spier became acting chair, responsible for finding replacements to cover Sapir's teaching—a difficult task to replace someone so famous. Spier wanted to maintain student enthusiasm for technical linguistic work within the Anthropology Department, and so he wrote to the hiring authorities: "Whorf has a very stimulating way, I think, and I would like to take advantage of his interest in hooking up language and ethnology, for I think it would take with many of our students. They might thus be encouraged to give serious attention to linguistics, when a "straight" linguistics course might leave them cold" (Darnell 1990, p. 81).

The course Whorf proposed was to cover "a number of languages, including Hopi, Aztec, Maya, other Uto-Aztecan languages, a Penurian language, and a survey of the rest . . . and a general discussion of language classification."[23] By all accounts the course was successful in interesting the anthropology students to understand the methods and results of linguistic analysis.

Many of the detractors of Whorfianism start by introducing him as "a fire insurance engineer and amateur linguist", thereby suggesting something unprofessional about his abilities in the field of Amerindian languages. In response we should remark (following Levinson, 2012, p. xiv, n. 3): "amateurism is not the right gloss for a man who published three or more scholarly papers a year, often in the top journals of his profession, taught at Yale, enjoyed the regard of the leading scholars of his day, and contributed enduring terminology to the discipline."

---

[22] The genetic problem concerns the grouping of different language types or families. These quotations are from Darnell (1990, p. 378).

[23] The Spier letter as well as the Whorf proposal are in Darnell (1990, pp. 380–381).

However, sometimes the detractors appear to have egregiously misread what Whorf actually wrote. An example is Pinker (1994, p. 60), who gives a list of three of Whorf's Amerindian sentences and criticizes them on two counts. He first claims that the three sentence examples were from the Apache language (Pinker attributes this claim to Eric Lenneberg or Roger Brown or both) but that Whorf never studied Apache or had a true Apache informant. In response to this, we remind the reader that we have already mentioned Whorf's paper on Chiricahua Apache in note 12, and we've noted that Vogelin considered Whorf "the best man for the genetic problem", which of course would include the Apache language. While it is true that Whorf never had an Apache informant or studied Apache intensively, the three sentences that Pinker produces are *not* Apache sentences, nor does Whorf label them so either in their published journal appearances or in Carroll (1956b); Carroll et al. (2012). The first two sentences (the boat and the feast examples) are from Nootka (Carroll, 1956b, pp. 236, 243; Carroll et al., 2012, pp. 302, 310), a language spoken in the Vancouver Islands; the third sentence (gun example) is in Shawnee (Carroll, 1956b, pp. 168–169, 208; Carroll et al., 2012, pp. 215–216, 267). And in fact, Whorf identifies them clearly in the text, and *did* study these two languages, as his text also makes clear. We discuss these sentences more fully in §3.7, as well as some further features of Hopi and other Amerindian languages.

Pinker's second criticism is that "Whorf rendered the sentences as clumsy, word-for-word translations, designed to make the literal meanings seem as odd as possible." This issue of appropriate translation is important and deep. We discuss it more in §§3.6.2–3.7.

3.6.2 Whorf and Malotki on Hopi Time

Many authors cite Malotki (1983) as evidence that Whorf's analysis of Hopi is fundamentally flawed. But in fact, what has become clear is that it is the researcher's predilection towards or against linguistic relativity that makes one or the other of Whorf's or Malotki's translations and analyses of certain linguistic phenomena seem correct to that researcher. Or perhaps they are both correct – for different purposes.

As we mentioned earlier, Whorf's main or only regular informant was Naquayouma, although as we also have mentioned, Whorf did go in person once to the Second Mesa to "confirm what [he] had transcribed from Naquayouma". Naquayouma was born in 1906, was raised in the traditional Hopi manner, and was the son of a chief. Those were the days before the widespread broadcast of radio, and before visits to the Mesa environments by non-Hopi were common. Naquayouma spoke as close to "pure" Hopi language as could be possible after the initial meetings with Spanish conquistadors and English-language immigrants. Malotki (1983) does not explicitly give the years that he spent on the Third Mesa, but he acknowledges that most of the linguistic input he collected was from "Michael Lomatewama of Hotvela and Herschel Talashoma from Paaqavi" and that "the dialect represented throughout this monograph is that spoken in the Third Mesa villages of Hotvela and Paaqavi by generally bilingual Hopi in ages ranging from the late thirties to the late seventies" (Malotki, 1983, p. ix). He also, a bit later (Malotki, 1983, p. 7), says that these men's speech habits represented an earlier time: their speech was "marked by certain phonological and morphological traits that are no longer practiced by speakers of the latest generation".

Dinwoodie (2006, pp. 336–341) presents a detailed look at the evidence Malotki used in analyzing the Hopi ceremonial system of the Wuwtsim; Whorf had claimed to have found in this ceremony no evidence of "time as we [SAE speakers] know it", but Malotki translated this ceremony using SAE time references. The best that could be asserted, Dinwoodie claimed, was that Malotki demonstrated that "inserting the English term *time* into the translations of four sentences of unknown provenance does not render them entirely unintelligible."

How should we evaluate the correctness of a translation – say, from Hopi to English? One might ask a native speaker of Hopi, but of course if such a speaker is a monolingual Hopi speaker, this won't help. If the speaker is Hopi/English bilingual, we will get an answer (as Whorf got from Naquayouma and Malotki got from Lomatewama and Talashoma), but its accuracy will always be in question because the influence of learning the one language (English) after the other (Hopi) is a highly interfering parameter. Another way – one that Whorf appeals to often – is to examine the grammatical categories of the

Hopi expressions and try to translate while preserving the grammatical category, often at the cost of generating a "non-natural-sounding" translation. But this also will be questioned: what independent reason can be given for choosing such a "bad-sounding" translation? Such a choice is always in the forefront of an act of translation: if one is translating a literary work from language L_1 into language L_2, the goal is to make the translation appear as "natural" in L_2 as it was in L_1, and this will often amount to changes in the linguistic categories of the items of L_1, as for example in the examples cited just below. But if one wished to exhibit the linguistic structure of a sentence, perhaps with the idea that this structure will say something about how the language's speakers view reality, one might get an "awkward" or even "ungrammatical" version in L_2.[24] Even in closely related members of SAE languages this can appear. Consider German, French, and Italian in (a), translated into English in (b) with the idea of keeping syntactic/semantic features constant, versus (c) which, is more "natural" in English.

(a) Claudia sah viele Blitze.
François a beaucoup de meubles.
Il barbiere ha tagliato i capelli a Gennaro.
(b) Claudia saw many lightnings.
François has many furnitures.
The barber cut Gennaro's hairs.
(c) Claudia saw much lightning.
François has a lot of furniture.
The barber cut Gennaro's hair.

These are merely examples of a difference of the mass/count feature of nouns between English and German/French/Italian. Some, translating into English while maintaining the syntactic structures of the

---

[24] Mithun, 1990, p. 310) remarks "If the investigation of grammatical structures were limited to data consisting of isolated sentences translated from a contact language like English, much would be missed. Translations can easily distort the grammatical patterns of a language in ways that obscure their actual functions: Too often, aspects of the language under investigation are understood as perfect counterparts to their translations when in fact they are parts of very different systems."

original, as in (b), might wish to say that German, French, and Italian speakers "conceptualize" lightning, furniture, and hair as groups of separate "entities", whereas English speakers think of lightning, furniture, and hair as "stuff": undifferentiated, and (presumably) thereby uncountable. On the other hand, those who translate the sentences into "natural English", as in (c), would wish to say that there is no "real conceptual difference" between the German/French/Italian speakers and the English.

Not only *might* Whorf draw the inference to a difference in conceptualization with regard to mass and count nouns, with respect to English versus Hopi, he in fact *does* draw that inference. He distinguishes count from mass terms, saying that "count nouns denote bodies with definite outlines", while "mass nouns denote homogeneous continua without implied boundaries." Since, as he says, "rather few natural occurrences present themselves as unbounded extents" and instead we experience "bodies small or large with definite outlines", this forces English speakers to find "some way of individualizing the mass noun", which is "partly done by names of body-types: 'stick of wood, piece of cloth, pane of glass, cake of soap... glass of water, cup of coffee." This "inconvenience" forces SAE speakers to posit "the philosophic [distinction of] 'substance' vs. 'matter," as if they were "common sense." But Hopi, Whorf claims, is different: there is a class of nouns, but "no formal subclass of mass nouns. All nouns have an individual sense and both singular and plural forms." Hopi nouns that most closely translate our mass nouns do imply indefiniteness of boundaries, but *not* a lack of boundary: they imply indefiniteness of size and outline. "In specific statements, 'water' means one certain mass or quantity of water, not what we call 'the substance water'. Generality of statement is conveyed through the verb or predicator, not the noun." "One says, not 'a glass of water' but $kə\cdot yi$ 'a water,' ... not 'a piece of meat' but sik^wi 'a meat'. The language has neither need for or analogies on which to build the concept of existence of a duality of formless item and forms. It deals with formlessness through other symbols than nouns" (Whorf's cited remarks are from Whorf (1941b). See Carroll(1956b), pp. 134–159; Carroll *et al.* (2012), pp. 174–204).

A similar example of this sort of "translation preference" is raised in Lee (1991), where she cites Whorf as having this view

Hopi has abundant conjugational and lexical means of expressing duration, intensity, and tendency directly as such, ... various linguistic terms came supplied with *intensities* – their designations of duration, tendencies, and relative time position is "fused with intensity". The degree or strength of intensity amount to "distinctions of degree, rate, constancy, repetition, increase and decrease of intensity, immediate sequence, interruption or sequence after an interval, etc., also QUALITIES of strengths, such as we should express metaphorically as smooth, even, hard, rough. A striking feature is their lack of resemblance to the terms of real space and movement that to us "mean the same." There is not even more than a trace of apparent derivation from space terms. Whorf (1941b) [Carroll, 1956, p. 146; Carroll *et al*, 2012, p. 188]

Whorf further remarks that the "use of space terms when there is no space involved" is simply not present in Hopi, and this is due to the presence of the "abundant conjugational and lexical means of expressing duration, intensity, and tendency directly as such, and that major grammatical patterns do not, as with us, provide analogies for an imaginary space."

Of this, Lee (1991, p. 127) says: "while on the one hand, we can think of human activity as taking place in a container-like frame made up of spatial and temporal parameters which can be separately measured, we can also think of it . . . as being impregnated with spatio-temporality expressed in terms of repetition, sequence, constancy, duration, tendency, relative temporal relations, and a range of other indices to which we pay attention as we make meaning out of complexes of experiential data".

Lee distinguishes Malotki's and Whorf's treatments of Hopi grammar along these separate lines:

Malotki (1983) has conceptualized space and time as separate, differentiating spatial contexts and temporal contexts. He has argued that many locatives and adverbials in Hopi are basically spatial in semantic import, but are used metaphorically to communicate temporal information. By contrast, Whorf thought that the Hopi operate in a fused space/time conceptual universe ... where space and time interpenetrate. Those locatives and adverbials which seem ambiguous are not so by this way of thinking, because they operate in a total spatio-temporal context where metaphor is not required. He said that the "Hopi conceive time and motion in the objective realm in a purely operational sense – a matter of the complexity and magnitude of operations connecting events – so that the element of time is not separated from whatever element of space enters into the operations". (Lee, 1991, p. 127)

A significant aspect of these differing viewpoints on translating Hopi (as well as other American Indian languages) into some SAE language is due to the difference between "polysynthetic" and "synthetic" languages (the latter including "analytic" languages). The former style of language can be seen as favouring the modification of some verbal description, whereas the latter style identifies the objects and actors independently of the action being asserted to occur. In §3.7 we follow up with comments relevant to these features of Hopi (and others of the American Indian languages).

Similar, but perhaps more careful, remarks are made by Hinton (1988) in her review of Malotki:

> ... the real disagreement between Whorf and Malotki is not whether time and space are linked, but instead whether the link is *metaphorical* in Hopi or whether they are simply not separable concepts at all. Whorf did recognize the close link between the English concept of time and the Hopi concept of space.[25] ... It is obvious from these quotes that Whorf was well-aware of the link between space and time in Hopi thought.
>
> Malotki never wrestles with the problem of defining the basis of the concept of "time," either universally or language-specifically. Instead, he makes the error of attributing temporality to any Hopi

---

[25] Hinton's three quotes from Whorf (p. 363) are:
[Hopi does not] refer to space in such a way as to exclude that element of extension or existence that we call 'time'. (Carroll 1956, p. 57)
...DISTANCE includes what we call 'time' in the sense of the temporal relation between events which have already happened. (Carroll 1956, p. 63)
Both the 'here' happening and the 'there' happening are in the objective, corresponding in general to our past, but the 'there' happening is the more objective distant, meaning, from our standpoint, that it is further away in the past just as it is further away from us in space than the 'here' happening (Carroll 1956, p. 63)

sentence that translates into English with a temporal term. One example is a Hopi sentence that translates "I did it three times";[26] literally, this sentence should translate more along the lines of "I did three repetitions." It is questionable as to whether such usage of the word "time" in English should be viewed as temporal at all. It might be argued that this usage in English is a metaphor, or perhaps, a metonymy, where the notion that events are bounded in time is taken as representation of the event itself. There is no evidence in the Hopi sentence of such metonymy; it is simply not a temporal sentence. (Hinton, 1988, p. 363)

Hinton continues with various other examples where she complains about Malotki's choice to use the word *time* in a translation where, she says, "there is no reason to assume that the Hopi sentence is dealing with a notion of temporality at all" and "Malotki does not satisfactorily separate Hopi views of time from the views expressed by English translations. What is *meant* by the word 'time', and what are the criteria for determining whether or not a concept is 'temporal'? These are very difficult issues which were central to Whorf's concerns, but are not grappled with deeply in Malotki's work."

As a final comment on the Whorf-Malotki dispute, we note that Dinwoodie (2006) also draws attention to the two epigraphs that appear on the opening cover page of Malotki (1983, p. vii). The first is from Whorf (1936; Carroll, 1956b, p. 57; Carroll et al., 2012, p. 73), and the second is the English translation Malotki provides of a part of the Wuwtsim story:

After a long and careful study and analysis, the Hopi language is seen to contain no words, grammatical forms, constructions or expressions that refer directly to what we call "time," ...

Then indeed, the following day, quite early in the morning at the hour when people pray to the sun, around the time when he woke up the girl again.

---

[26] Apparently the occurrence of the cited sentence is in Malotki (1983, p. 512), although the sentence *payi-s-tota* is translated as 'They did it three times' by Malotki.

Dinwoodie remarks: "We are apparently to see that the second epigraph provides a direct challenge to the first. Chock full, as it seems to be, with 'references' to 'time,' the second passage is meant to leave the reader wondering, why, as Malotki puts it, 'Whorf erred so drastically.' (Malotki, 1983, p. 631). What draws our attention, however, is that the second passage is attributed *not to a Hopi individual* but to 'Ekkhart Malotki, Hopi Field Notes 1980'"(Dinwoodie, 2006, p.346fn5).

The lack of any native speakers of the classical version of Hopi ensures that we will never be able to evaluate empirically the correctness or incorrectness of Whorf's work versus Malotki's work on this topic. But one thing seems certain: it is simply wrong to say that Malotki's work is obviously a crushing demolition of Whorf's analysis. It is more accurate to say that anyone's strategy in translation will have to beg the question one way or the other: if a translation from L_1 to L_2 maintains what are acknowledged to be the very different syntactic features of L_1 then it will *of course* sound exotic or even just a bad translation to speakers of L_2; but if it is made to sound "normal" in L_2, then *of course* it will obliterate any claim of "wondrous novelty" to speakers of L_1, when made by speakers of L_2. It seems natural to identify this dispute as a feature of emic-theories of linguistic relativity: this is all contained within the linguistic realm, without appeal to how the alleged "language internal" features give rise to any behavioural differences.

3.6.3 Greenberg on Whorf

As we have mentioned earlier, the phrase "The Sapir-Whorf Hypothesis" was not very commonly used (if at all) until a conference organized by Harry Hoijer held in 1953. Apparently, the first published use of the term was as the title of the paper by Hoijer at that conference (Hoijer, 1954b), although presumably in his formal and informal invitations to other participants he might have also used the term. The actual title of the conference was "Language in Culture", and the proceedings of the conference were published as (Hoijer, 1954a). In the introduction to the published proceedings, Hoijer (1954a, p. vii),

Hoijer says "the conference was proposed originally by Robert Redfield". There were seven papers prepared for the conference, which were distributed to the 20 invited participants in advance. The discussions were recorded and (mostly) transcribed for the published record of the conference, as a set of nine "discussion sessions".

Relevant to the present discussion of Whorf's account of Hopi time is a section of Joseph Greenberg's contribution Greenberg, 1954 in which he discusses translation, in particular the topic of "the choice of an equivalent from another language, normally that of the writer, ... for inferences of similarity [of translation meaning]. This is the process which underlies the uncritical use of literal translation frequently encountered in the literature. It can be seen that this procedure is quite arbitrary inasmuch as interpretation of the same data will differ, depending on the particular language employed for translation" (Greenberg, 1954, pp. 13–14).

Greenberg cites as an example Whorf's reasoning regarding the Hopi use of cardinal and ordinal numbers. Both English and Hopi have two sets of numeral types; but, while there is considerable overlap in situations where the two languages use cardinals and where they use ordinals, there is a discrepancy in the *exact* places where the two languages will employ them. And thus Whorf concludes that the use of the Hopi ordinal when stating the number of days a duration takes justifies the conclusion that the Hopi do not view a succession of days as if they were a set of different days (a cardinal reading) but rather as a day recurring successively (an ordinal reading). But this is a faulty inference, Greenberg says, and lampoons it thus:

> Employing the same reasoning, a Frenchman who calls his kings Henri quatre (*Henry four*) and Louis treize (*Louis thirteen*) might draw the conclusion that English speakers who use the phrases "Henry the fourth" and "Louis the thirteenth" view each king of the same name as the same man appearing anew. He might even conjecture a belief in reincarnation of like-named kings. Further, a French observer might even be moved to conclusions similar those entertained by Whorf for Hopi regarding the English conceptualization of time periods, by contrasting the French Juillet quatorze (*July fourteen*) with English "July fourteenth." On the other hand,

the German metalinguist accustomed to Heinrich der vierte (*Henry the fourth*) and der vierzehnte Juli (*the fourteenth July*) would not have a basis for drawing conclusions similar to that of the French scientist concerning the English-speaking community. (Greenberg, 1954, p. 14)

Clearly, there is an important issue here about translation. And it is not at all clear how one should address the issue of when a translation is appropriate to a certain end – whether it is to be "a natural way of talking" in the language being translated into, or is to "respect the syntactic and semantic categories" of the language being translated from. But for evaluating the truth or falsity of linguistic relativity – or (more weakly) the appropriateness of attributing differing worldviews to speakers of importantly different languages, or (even more weakly) the denial of "universalism" of human language acquisition – one will need to take a stand on this issue.

3.7 American Indian Languages: Whorfian Understandings of Structure

There are various ways to categorize the world's languages: one might look to a language's

(a) "standard word order" (Subject-Verb-Object vs. Subject-Object-Verb vs. Verb-Object-Subject vs. . . .),
(b) "patterns of sound systems" (relative frequencies of phonological features, such as voicing contrasts in stops but not fricatives, etc.)
(c) number of different sounds employed (number of consonants, number of vowels, number of complex consonants like clicks, lateral affricates, uvular consonants, etc.)
(d) "morphological structures" (how the language forms words by combining morphemes)

Of interest to the present discussion is the last-mentioned method of categorization: morphology, which was a method either invented or at least popularized by Sapir (1921). A morpheme is the smallest "lexical item" in a given language: words (except for "compound words"), but also affixes that are only found in combination with other morphemes, for example, the prefix *un-* or the plural suffix *-s* in English. Even though these factors occur along a spectrum among the world's language, it is standard to categorize languages as

- Analytic: most morphemes are words. There are very few affixes. These languages rely on word order and auxiliary words to convey meanings. (Examples: Classical Chinese [of the time of Confucius]; to a lesser extent, modern Mandarin; to an even lesser extent, English)
- Synthetic: basically = nonanalytic; divided into three types:
  - Agglutinative: words contain several distinct morphemes that have a unique and clearly different meanings from one another. (Example: Swahili)
  - Fusional: morphemes are not easily distinguishable from the root element; several aspects of meaning may be fused into one affix; often affixes manifest as internal phonological changes in the root word. (Example: Spanish, German, various other European languages)
  - Polysynthetic: the root is normally verbal, but in a sentence there are normally a very large number of morphemes that correspond to many argument positions besides the subject. It is generally the case that polysynthetic languages feature entire sentences as single words (or rather: a single word can be equivalent to an entire sentence in other languages).[27] (Examples: Finnish, most Native American languages of the northwest coastal region)

(It should be noted that these categories admit of degrees, and thus merge into one another.)

Now, a great many of the American Indian languages are polysynthetic,[28] where the normal utterance of a sentence amounts to a single

---

[27] The "bible" for polysynthesis is Baker (1995), even though it is written within the "Principles and Parameters" phase of Chomsky's development.

[28] A small sample of citations where descriptions of the unique phenomena surrounding such languages are explained: Sapir and Swadish (1946); Hukari (1976); Kinkade

word – a verb that encodes all the syntactic relationships among the various items that would be called "nouns" in other types of languages by means of having agreement with certain aspects of the verb. We thus turn to the issue of translation of sentences in these languages when all the syntactic relationships among the various "nouns" are presented by means of having agreement with certain aspects of the verb. In his "Languages and Logic," the third of Whorf's *Technology Review* works (Whorf, 1941a), he cites the sentence *tlih-is-ma* of the Nootka language of Vancouver Island (the hyphens separate the various aspects). About this Nootka sentence he says (Carroll, 1956b, p. 236; Carroll et al., 2012, pp. 302–303): "... the final *-ma* is only the sign of the third-person indicative. [This sentence does not] contain any unit of meaning akin to our word 'boat' or even 'canoe'. [The first part] means 'moving pointwise,' i.e., moving in a way like [Whorf's drawing of the wake of a boat], hence 'traveling in or as a canoe,' or an event like one position of such motion. It is not a name for what we should call a "thing," but is more like a vector in physics. [The second part] means 'on the beach', hence *thil-is-ma* means 'it is on the beach pointwise as an event of canoe motion' ..."

As Whorf says, we English-speakers might wish to translate the sentence *tlih-is-ma* as "The canoe is landed on the beach". But giving such a translation just does not honour the way the sentence is formed, and (at least to Whorf and his followers) does not adequately capture the "flavour" or "intent" or "views of the world" that the Nootka speakers of the sentence have. For no boat is mentioned in that sentence, only canoe motion that implies a boat. As we mentioned in §3.6.2, there is a "forced choice" in translation styles: the translator either tries to illustrate the syntactic-semantic structure of the to-be-translated sentence in the language the sentence is being translated into, or the translator ignores that and somehow comes up with how the original might be most naturally said in the language being translated into. In the

(1983); Jelinek (1993); Jelinek and Demers (1994); Bach (1994, 1995, 2007); Jelinek (1995). Hopi is a very special case. See Gronemeyer (1996) for a discussion of the position of Hopi on the polysynthetic "curve". He concludes (p. 41): "Hopi displays a number of polysynthetic structures but lacks certain key features such as free word order and free pro-drop. Rather than explain away these polysynthetic properties, I suggest that the Polysynthesis Parameter does apply in Hopi, but that its effects are partially obscured due to some other macro- or microparameter applying at a more superficial level".

act of translating from L_1 into L_2, Whorf always chooses the former, and then remarks on how the presumed event or other "reality" being described by his translation is different from the way speakers of L_2 might view it. But many critics choose the latter and then criticize the translation by a follower of Whorf as clumsy or otherwise inadequate.

A little later in the same article (Carroll, 1956b, p. 242; Carroll et al., 2012, p. 311), Whorf gives another Nootka sentence, *tl'imshya'isita'itlma*, which he characterizes as "a simple, not a complex, Nootka sentence." (He also remarks that "Nootka has no parts of speech, the simplest utterance is a sentence, treating of some event or event-complex. Long sentences are sentences of sentences (complex sentences), not just sentences of words" – mirroring the characterization of polysyntheticity we have given.) About this sentence he says: "it begins with the event of 'boiling or cooking,' *tl'imsh*; then comes *-ya* ('result') = ('cooked'); then *-'is* 'eating' = 'eating cooked food', then *-ita* ('those who do') = ('eaters of cooked food'); then *-'itl* ('going for'), then *-ma*, sign of third-person indicative"

He follows this by claiming that a crude English paraphrase would be 'he, or somebody, goes for (invites) eaters of cooked food' (or perhaps in more natural English: 'He invites people to a feast.') Whorf is here concerned to show that the Nootka sentence is not divisible into the subject and predicate, or actor and object, relations that are essential in English. Or as he puts it (Carroll, 1956b, p. 241; Carroll et al., 2012, p. 309):

> The Indo-European languages and many others give great prominence to a type of sentence having two parts, each part built around a class of word – substantives and verbs – which those languages treat differently in grammar.... This distinction is not drawn from nature; it is just a result of the fact that every tongue must have some kind of structure.... The Greeks, especially Aristotle, built up this contrast and made it a law of reason. Since then, the contrast has been stated in logic in many different ways: subject and predicate, actor and action, things and relations between things, objects and their attributes, quantities and operation. And, pursuant again to grammar, the notion became ingrained that one of these classes of entities

can exist in its own right but that the verb class cannot exist without an entity of the other class, the "thing" class, as a peg to hang on.

And for Whorf, the Nootka language shows that this is just not true: in Nootka, only the verb exists.

But of course, Nootka is not the only polysynthetic language in the Americas. Much effort has been expended in studying the Salishan languages of southwestern British Columbia and northwestern Washington. Emmon Bach (1994, pp. 273–274), remarks:

> the Salishan language Samish (or Straits Salish), lacks a contrast between nouns and verbs, ... it is an example of a kind of language ... [where] there are simply no predicates in the sense of this essay. What appear to be predicates are in fact logically full sentences or formulas, which contain pronominal arguments (perhaps phonologically null). Such languages do not have full Noun Phrase (term phrase) arguments at all. Rather, the NP's that appear in sentences are to be understood as adjuncts, appositive amplifications of the minimal content given by the pronominal argument of the verbal element in the sentence. Here are some examples ...
> *Cey ce sweyqe* "He-works, the (one who is a) man"
> *Sweyqe ce cey* "He (is a) man, the (one-who) works"

And Kinkade (1983, p. 25) remarks: "only predicates and particles can be distinguished. ... But whether looked at morphologically, syntactically, semantically, or logically, and whether at a surface or deep level, the notions noun and verb (as well as other traditional parts of speech) are not relevant in Salish. A Salishan sentence contains at least a predicate, which may be inflected for pronominal subject and/or object (as well as aspect, control, transitivity, etc.). An overt subject or object may be expressed by adding another predicate in apposition to the pronominal elements affixed to the main predicate".

This has the effect of saying that such languages can have sentences that are single words, and that they can encode all the syntactic relationships among the various "nouns" by having agreement with certain aspects of the verb. Further, many such languages allow for an inflection of the verb to achieve the same end as adverbs and adjectives in SAE languages. And thus in the Salishian languages (as well as other polysynthetic languages) there is no noun-verb distinction.[29]

But it might be asked: what does this radical departure of the grammatical features of polysynthetic languages from those of the various SAE languages really say about the Sapir-Whorf hypothesis? Is there any point at which the behaviours of (say) Salishian speakers differ from those of German speakers who might find themselves in the same situation? And even if there is a difference in behaviour, can it be shown that this difference is caused by the difference in their languages' syntactic styles? This brings us back, once again, to the topic we first encountered in Chapter 1 and have mentioned at various places since then: the emic/etic distinction, to which we return in Chapter 4.

---

[29] We should mention that there is also a backlash reaction to this claim, forcefuly put forth by van Eijk and Hess (1986), who sum up their position thus (p. 329):

> "In summation, we can say that there are two basic word-classes in Salish and these classes are similar enough to the 'noun' and 'verb' in Indo-European to apply profitably in descriptions of Salish. The traditional criterion by which nouns are distinguished from verbs (viz., the idea that nouns are typically complements in a predication while verbs are typically predicates) fails for Salish, since in Salish both nouns and verbs freely serve in both predicates and complements." As we see, even this claim allows that there is no predicate-versus-argument distinction being made between the proposed classes, which seems to be the main point of Whorf's (as well as Bach's) claims.

4
Three Interpretations of Linguistic Relativity

It has been pointed out by many commentators that Whorf's (and Sapir's) writings on Whorfianism did not suggest that ethnographers and linguists should look into speakers' brains—either directly nor indirectly through behaviour—for "scientifically acceptable, empirical proof" of instances of linguistic relativity, or of the more general notion of linguistic relativity in brains. Possibly that was because they were not experimental scientists, and possibly because the "cognitive turn" in linguistics had not yet occurred, and possibly because it was not clear to those interested in linguistic relativity what sort of evidence could even be relevant, over and above the demonstrated "deep differences among languages".

As we also mentioned much earlier, neither Whorf nor Sapir used the term 'hypothesis' – the phrase *The Sapir-Whorf Hypothesis* dates from the period of the conference that led to the publication of Hoijer (1954a), more than a decade after their deaths.

Given that the phrase doesn't occur in either Sapir or Whorf, it should not be very surprising that neither of them treated their findings as a touchstone for definitively testing whether some well-defined state of language will have such-and-so particular (type of) effect on the culture or on actions of any individual speakers. And so we might conclude, along with Lee (1996, p. 84), that the notion of a scientific hypothesis was never in their minds. It would be better described, as Lee puts it, as "The Sapir-Whorf relativity *principle*", and not a hypothesis.

The 1950s saw a turn towards emphasizing the issue of empirically testing linguistic relativity, as we will discuss in the next section. But parallel with this new emphasis was a continuation of the idea of Whorfianism as a "relativity *principle*". The very interesting anthology by Pütz and Verspoor (2000) consists mostly of authors who advocate this latter view of Whorfianism, to the surprise of Jürgen Bohnemeyer, who remarked in his (2002) review:

> When the cognitive revolution began to change the fields of psychology, linguistics, and anthropology in the 1950s, it also stimulated a reinterpretation of relativism. The hallmark of this new approach to relativism was an emphasis on effects of language on *non-linguistic* cognition, and consequently an emphasis on experimental psychological evidence. ... It is surprising, then, that most contributors to [Pütz and Verspoor, 2000] propose, address, and advocate or criticize a view of relativism that disagrees with the cognitivist interpretation. For example, the case studies seek evidence for or against possible Whorfian effects entirely within the linguistic sphere. That is, they assume that such effects originate from linguistic categories (e.g. color or kinship terms; a Bantu noun class; an English metaphor) and manifest themselves in linguistic behavior (i.e. the use and extension of these categories), without attempting to test non-linguistic cognition. (p. 453–454)

And Bohnemeyer continues with a "chart" that outlines the important differences that would distinguish the two viewpoints on linguistic relativism:

Noncognitivist views of relativism

1. Relativism is a program: Given that language influences thought, how are we to study language, culture, and cognition in view of relativism?
2. Relativism presupposes a view of the mind in which language is a modality of thought (possibly the only one); nonlinguistic cognition is outside the scope of relativism.
3. Separation of linguistic and psychological evidence misses the point, making us overlook the primary effects of language on thought.
4. The primary effects of language on thought are expected to show up in categorizaton—conceptual categories are determined by (or are the same as) linguistic categories.

Cognitivist views of relativism

1. Relativism is an empirically testable hypothesis.
2. Language and nonlinguistic cognition can be studied independently of each other. The question is: does language influence nonlinguistic cognition?
3. Empirical testing should proceed by assessing language structure/use independently of cognitive representations, and then looking for alignments.
4. Languages impose codability constraints on cognitive representations, which are expected to manifest themselves in memory, attention, cospeech gesture, and representational formats.

Bohnemeyer's comparison of two viewpoints should call to mind the emic/etic distinction we first mentioned in Chapter 1 and referenced at various points of this book between that section and here (and which we will discuss even further a little later in this book). Bohnemeyer's points of comparison seem to be natural consequences of the characterization we gave earlier of emic and etic: namely, that an emic study of an anthropological/sociological feature is done "from within the society" whereas an etic study is done "from the viewpoint of an observer or outside investigator of the society". Consequently, an emic study requires the investigator to be in (or, at least, convincingly put him/herself into) the society under investigation. One must be able to adopt the cultural beliefs and worldview, as well as the language, and on that basis draw conclusions about the relationships between these aspects and which aspects of one are responsible for beliefs of another of them. This doesn't quite sit comfortably with all of Bohnemeyer's dicta, but it does seem to capture the intent: an investigator somehow needs to insert him- or herself into the daily life (and language) of the subject society and then investigate how that embedding affects such mental operations as categorization: both mental categorization and linguistic categorization.

It is not so clear that this is really possible. It seems that such an investigator would need to have feet in two camps: the subject culture and the investigating culture; the subject's language and the investigator's language. But even that fortuitous circumstance wouldn't tell us what the monolinguist subject's thought was, but rather what such thought was when it was "contaminated" by the investigator's language.

4.1 Is Linguistic Relativity Empirically Testable?

Although it may have been that Sapir and Whorf were "noncognitivist" in their opinions, and perhaps were advocates of an emic position in their claims about what linguistic relativity was, the history of thought concerning linguistic relativity didn't really evolve in that direction. Instead, there was argumentation, beginning especially around the time of the Hoijer conference, concerning the extent to which linguistic relativity was "a really testable principle in the scientific sense." And as certain early results seemed (to some) to show "relevant linguistic effects"—mostly in the colour domain, and mostly, it seemed, not very striking—there started to be a feeling among linguists (predominantly) and ethnographers (to a lesser extent) that there wasn't very much at all to linguistic relativity. A standard dichotomy that reflected this opinion was apparently first named in Penn (1972): "Strong Whorfianism versus Weak Whorfianism" (although Penn usually called the Strong version "Extreme" and the Weak version "Mild").[1] Among the alleged consequences of Strong Whorfianism was the claim that language and thought were identical. And that this would require "an extra-human source of language". Penn (1972, p. 55), also thinks that, historically, "the extreme hypothesis may have been offered as an antidote to the assumption of innate ideas, because the mild hypothesis, while easier to support and defend, would not have as effectively countered the notion that we are all born with a certain set of cognitive abilities." But the received attitude—especially by those not involved directly in the debate—seems to be that Strong ("extreme") Hypothesis is completely implausible while the Weak ("mild") Hypothesis is too trivial to debate ("of course one's language has *some* influence on how you think; no one ever thought otherwise").

---

[1] Prior to 1972, there were plenty of remarks about different ways to understand Whorfianism. But it was Penn's work that popularized this particular way of drawing the distinction.

4.2 Constructing (and Evaluating) "Scientific" Relativistic Hypotheses

The 1950s–1980s (and still continuing 40 years later) saw an ever-increasing number of attempts to formulate "scientific" verifications or refutations of linguistic relativity. These attempts to investigate the scientific standing of linguistic relativity were a part of the so-called cognitive revolution that was initiated in the 1950s, and they were concerned to establish (or rebut)—in a "scientifically acceptable" way—the effects of language on nonlinguistic cognition. This interpretation of linguistic relativity included a strong emphasis on psychological experimentation and the interpretation of psychological evidence. If one is tempted by this understanding of linguistic relativity, then (following standard experimentation norms) there are a number of considerations that are relevant to formulating, testing, and evaluating Whorfian hypotheses.

Genuine hypotheses of this "scientific" type that concern the effects of language on thought will always have a duality: there will be a linguistic part and a nonlinguistic one. The linguistic part will involve a claim that some feature is present in one language but absent in another.

Whorf himself conjectured that it was only obligatory features of languages that established "mental patterns" or "habitual thought" (Carroll, 1956a, pp. 139-140f; Carroll et al., 2012, pp. 179-181), and when one thinks of it, it seems clear that if a feature is optional then the speaker will *not* necessarily have the relevant (yet coerced) "mental pattern" or "habitual thought". So, we will also restrict our attention to obligatory features here. (In addition, if linguists discovered that some linguistic feature was optional in both languages, then even if psychological experiments showed differences between the two populations of speakers, this would not show linguistic determination or influence. The cognitive differences might depend on (say) cultural differences.)

Examples of relevant obligatory features would include lexical distinctions like the light versus dark blue forced choice in Greek and Russian, or the forced choice between "in (fitting tightly)" versus "in (fitting loosely)" in Korean. They also include grammatical distinctions like the forced choice in Spanish second-person pronouns between informal/intimate and formal/distant (informal *tú* vs.

formal *usted* in the singular; informal *vosotros* vs. formal *ustedes* in the plural) or the forced choice in Tagalog first-person plural pronouns between inclusive ("*tayo* = me and you and perhaps others") and exclusive ("*kami* = me and others not including you"). (A similar distinction holds in very many other languages.) They might also include forced choices of grammatical gender and its possible interaction with natural gender. One of Whorf's often-mentioned differences between various American languages and SAE languages concerned different systems of tense, and how these might affect some behaviour.

The nonlinguistic part of a Whorfian hypothesis will contrast the psychological effects that habitually using the two languages has on their speakers. For example, one might conjecture that the habitual use of Spanish induces its speakers to be sensitive to the formal and informal character of the speaker's relationship with their interlocutor, while habitually using English does not.

So testing Whorfian hypotheses requires testing two independent hypotheses with the appropriate kinds of data. In consequence, evaluating them requires the expertise of both linguistics and psychology, and is a multidisciplinary enterprise. Clearly, the linguistic hypothesis may hold up where the psychological hypothesis does not, or conversely.

A further important consideration concerns the strength of the inducement relationship that a Whorfian hypothesis posits between a speaker's language and their nonlinguistic capacities. The claim that your language shapes or influences your cognition is quite different from the claim that your language makes certain kinds of cognition impossible (or obligatory) for you. The strength of any Whorfian hypothesis will vary depending on the kind of relationship being claimed, and the ease of revisability of that relation.

A testable Whorfian hypothesis will have a schematic form something like this:

> *Linguistic part*: Feature F is obligatory in L_1 but optional (or perhaps not present) in L_2.
> *Psychological part*: Speaking a language with obligatory feature F bears relation R to the cognitive effect C.

The relation R might in principle be causation or determination, but it is important to see that it might merely be correlation, or slight favouring; and the nonlinguistic cognitive effect C might be readily suppressible or revisable.

Dan Slobin (1996) presents a view that competes with Whorfian hypotheses as standardly understood. He hypothesizes that *when the speakers are using their cognitive abilities in the service of a linguistic ability* (speaking, writing, translating, etc.), the language they are planning to use to express their thought will have a temporary online effect on how they express their thought. ("Thinking for speaking" as Slobin puts it.) The claim is that as long as language users are thinking in order to frame their speech or writing or translation in some language, the mandatory features of that language will influence the way they think.

On Slobin's view, these effects quickly attenuate as soon as the activity of thinking for speaking ends. For example, if a speaker is thinking for writing in Spanish, then Slobin's hypothesis would predict that given the obligatory formal/informal second-person pronoun distinction they would pay greater attention to the formal/informal character of their social relationships with their audience than if they were writing in English. But this effect is not permanent. As soon as they stop thinking for speaking, the effect of Spanish on their thought ends.

Slobin's non-Whorfian linguistic relativist hypothesis raises the importance of psychological research on bilinguals or people who currently use two or more languages with a native or near-native facility. This is because one clear way to test Slobin-like hypotheses relative to Whorfian hypotheses would be to find out whether language-correlated nonlinguistic cognitive differences between speakers holds for bilinguals only when they are thinking for speaking in one language, and not when they are thinking for speaking in some other language. If the relevant cognitive differences appeared and disappeared depending on which language speakers were planning to express themselves in, it would go some way to vindicate Slobin-like hypotheses over more traditional Whorfian hypotheses. Of course, one could alternately accept a broadening of Whorfian hypotheses to include Slobin-like evanescent effects. Either way, attention must be paid to the persistence and revisability of the linguistic effects, if Slobin is right.

Grammatical gender is obligatory in the languages in which it occurs and has been claimed by Whorfians to have persistent and enduring nonlinguistic effects on representations of objects (Boroditsky et al., 2003). Kousta et al. (2008, p. 843) show that "for bilinguals there is intraspeaker relativity in semantic representations and, therefore, [grammatical] gender does not have a conceptual, non-linguistic effect." However, Kousta et al. support the claim that bilinguals' semantic representations vary depending on which language they are using, and thus will have transient effects. This suggests that although some semantic representations of objects may vary from language to language, their nonlinguistic cognitive effects are transitory. But other researchers have argued that there are deeper and more permanent effects associated with grammatical gender. We discuss this case later, in §4.5.

Some advocates of Whorfianism, as well as most anti-Whorfians, might hold that if Whorf-like hypotheses were true, then meaning would be globally and radically indeterminate. Thus, the truth of Whorfian hypotheses is equated with global linguistic relativism—which critics see as a self-undermining form of relativism.

But as we have shown, not all linguistic relativity hypotheses are global hypotheses: they are about what is induced by particular linguistic features. And the associated nonlinguistic perceptual and cognitive differences can be quite small, perhaps insignificant. For example, Winawer et al. (2007) investigated the way the forced lexical choice between light and dark blue in Russian (*siniy* vs. *goluboy*) plays out when speakers are asked to discriminate the two. They conclude:

> We found that Russian speakers were faster to discriminate two colors if they fell into different linguistic categories in Russian (one *siniy* and the other *goluboy*) than if the two colors were from the same category (both *siniy* or both *goluboy*). This category advantage was eliminated by a verbal, but not a spatial, dual task. Further, effects of language were most pronounced on more difficult, finer discriminations.[2] English speakers tested on the identical stimuli did

---

[2] Or as they put it in the detailed description of their results (p. 7783), "in near-color trials, the difference in the category advantage between no-interference and

not show a category advantage under any condition. These results demonstrate that categories in language can affect performance of basic perceptual color discrimination tasks. Further, they show that the effect of language is online, because it is disrupted by verbal interference. Finally, they show that color discrimination performance differs across language groups as a function of what perceptual distinctions are habitually made in a particular language. The case of the Russian blues suggests that habitual or obligatory categorial distinctions made in one's language result in language-specific categorical distortions in objective perceptual tasks. . . . The critical difference in this case is not that English speakers cannot distinguish between light and dark blues, but rather that Russian speakers cannot avoid distinguishing them: they must do so to speak Russian in a conventional manner. This communicative requirement appears to cause Russia speakers to habitually make use of this distinction even when performing a perceptual task that does not require language. (Winawer et al., 2007, pp. 7783–7784)

Their final conclusion about this case was: "the Whorfian question is often interpreted as a question of whether language affects nonlinguistic processes. Putting the question in this way presupposes that linguistic and nonlinguistic processes are highly dissociated in normal human cognition, such that many tasks are accomplished without the involvement of language. A different approach to the Whorfian question would be to ask the extent to which linguistic processes are normally involved when people engage in all kinds of seemingly nonlinguistic tasks. . . . Our results suggest that linguistic representations normally meddle in even surprisingly simple objective perceptual decisions" (Winawer et al., 2007, p. 7784).

On the other hand, though, even small effects can generate what seem to be more major behavioural change. For example, Thierry et al. (2009) describe a series of experiments that yield evidence that an

verbal-interference was significantly greater for Russian than English speakers. . . . Likewise, the difference in category advantage between spatial-interference and verbal-interference was significantly greater for Russian speakers than English speakers. . . No differences were observed for similar comparisons on far color trials."

obligatory lexical distinction between light and dark blue affects Greek speakers' colour perception in a unique way. The authors conclude:

> Our electrophysiological findings reveal not only an effect of the native language on implicit color discrimination as indexed by preattentive change detection but even electrophysiological differences occurring as early as 100 ms after stimulus presentation, a time range associated with activity in the primary and secondary visual cortices. We therefore demonstrate that language-specific distinctions between 2 colors affect early visual processing, even when color is task irrelevant. At debriefing, none of the participants highlighted the critical stimulus dimension tested (luminance) or reported verbalizing the colors presented to them. The findings of the present study establish that early stages of color perception are unconsciously affected by the terminology specific to the native language. They lend strong support to the Whorfian hypothesis by demonstrating, for the first time, differences between speakers of different languages in early stages of color perception beyond the observation of high-level categorization and discrimination effects strategically and overtly contingent on language-specific distinction. (Thierry et al., 2009, p. 4569)

The fact that Whorfian hypotheses need not be global linguistic relativist hypotheses means that they do not conflict with the claim that there are language universals. Structuralists of the first half of the twentieth century tended to disfavour the idea of universals: Martin Joos's characterization of structuralist linguistics as claiming that "languages can differ without limit as to either extent or direction" (Joos, 1966, p. 228) has been much quoted in this connection. If the claim that languages can vary without limit were conjoined with the claim that languages have significant and permanent effects on the concepts and worldview of their speakers, a truly profound global linguistic relativism would result. But neither conjunct should be accepted. Joos's remark is regarded by nearly all linguists today as overstated (and merely a caricature of the structuralists), and Whorfian hypotheses do not have to take a global or deterministic form. A form of "in-betweenness" for the colour data is offered by Regier et al. (2010):

We hope by now to have convinced the reader that she or he would be ill-advised to wholly back either the universalist or the relativist view of language and thought—and would be better off instead thinking outside the standard "universals versus relativity" framing. The traditional framing is simplistic, and hides interesting realities. One such reality is that at least in the color domain, there are clear universals governing the semantic distinctions that languages make—but there may also be some limited element of arbitrariness in exactly where category boundaries are drawn. This is an ultimately universalist finding, but with a relativist twist.... The second reality obscured—or at least left entirely unanticipated by the traditional framing—is that language may affect perception primarily in the right half of the visual field and much less if at all in the left half. These lateralized Whorf results—ultimately relativist this time, but again with a twist—reinforce the impression left by the review of color naming: The world is a more interestingly complicated place than is suggested by the options presented in the traditional framing of the debate. (p. 179)

And what seems to be a possibly "intermediate position" on the effect of differences in colour language on the psycho-physical underpinnings of colour perception, is presented by Roberson and Hanley (2010):

The evidence that we have reviewed in this chapter also points to the existence of distinct linguistic and nonlinguistic color systems. However, there is no evidence that the linguistic system is in any way superficial. Linguistic categorization in different languages and cultures partitions the same range of visible colors in different ways and these differences affect decisions about color even on visual search tasks. Evidence suggests that categorical effects in color perception and memory occur as a result of access to lexical codes for color in adults. Moreover, children appear to acquire adult-like patterns of discrimination and memory for color as soon as they learn the appropriate color terminology for their language and culture. Roberson and Hanley (2010, p. 194)

John Lucy, a conscientious and conservative researcher of Whorfian hypotheses, has remarked: "we still know little about the connections between particular language patterns and mental life—let alone how they operate or how significant they are... a mere handful of empirical studies address the linguistic relativity proposal directly and nearly all are conceptually flawed" (Lucy, 1996, p. 37).

Although further empirical studies on Whorfian hypotheses have been completed since Lucy published his 1996 review article, there has been dispute as to whether any of them have satisfied the criteria of:

— adequately utilizing both the relevant linguistic and psychological research,
— focusing on obligatory rather than optional linguistic features,
— stating hypotheses in a clear testable way, and
— ruling out relevant competing Slobin-like hypotheses.

There is much important work yet to be done on testing the range of Whorfian hypotheses and other forms of linguistic conceptual relativism, and on understanding the significance of any Whorfian hypotheses that turn out to be well supported. Hereafter we show some more recent work (including some involving John Lucy) that consciously tries to address such concerns and to incorporate these criteria.

One unfortunate consequence of the hegemony of English, Spanish, and Portuguese languages in the Americas is that there are no longer any monolingual groups of native speakers of the various American Indian languages that were the initial cause of the excitement of Boas, Sapir, Whorf, and the others and that led to the formulation of linguistic relativity.[3] The rather slight differences in behaviour that research has discovered among speakers of various languages (such as Greek and Russian, versus English and Spanish, for example) in the colour terms, or the differences that even closely related languages

---

[3] Wikipedia https://en.wikipedia.org/wiki/Hopi_language says that *Ethnologue* in 2015 reported there to be 7,350 Hopi, of whom 6,780 were native speakers (in the 2010 US census) but that only 40 were monolingual Hopi speakers in the 1990 survey. Presumably there are fewer than 40 now.

(e.g., English, French, German, Italian, for example) make about "which nouns are mass or count" or whether one uses "in (tightly)" versus "in (loosely)" just are not the sort of distinctions, nor do they call for the level of change in presumed mentation, that Whorf and the others claimed to detect in their studies of the American Indian languages.

4.3 *Should* Linguistic Relativity be Empirically Testable?: And If So, How? Emic and Etic Views of Theories of Language and of Its Effects

We think it fair to say that the interpretation of the results discovered by the very many who investigated the issue has depended to a rather large extent on whether one was or was not a "linguistic relativist" in the first place, and just what *kind* of relativist one was—cognitivist or some other variety. But let us once again discuss just what is involved in being "a linguistic relativist".

In §4.2 we described the relevant background to testing whether some relativist hypothesis is confirmable in a suitably "scientific" sense. We saw that there were two parts of such a test: a suitable linguistic difference between two languages, and a suitable (measurable) difference in the observable activities (etc.) of speakers of the two languages. In §4.4 we will rehearse a number of studies that stick close to that idea. But it will become clear that the (positive) differences that are discovered are minor, and often can be overturned by what seem to be mere force of will (or prior training) on the part of the subjects. And that in any case the findings seem not in themselves representative of any important difference in the lives (including mental lives) of the speakers of the different languages. We categorize these sorts of differences (on the assumption that they are genuine differences) as cases of "minor relativism". Perhaps it is true that the described linguistic differences generate differences in perception, action, and the like. But the areas are not of outstanding importance, and the differences are small ... even in those cases when the participants cannot alter their responses by "force of will". In our opinion, many of the cases described in §4.4 (and §4.2) report genuine relativistic results.

But they just are not all that interesting, except as an "existence proof" of effects of linguistic relativity that might open the doors to a receptivity of better/stronger relativistic evidence for cases of the sort we discuss in §4.5 and §4.6.

We also think that Penn's Strong/Weak ("extreme/mild") characterization of a bifurcation between which different types of Whorfianism might vary is not an adequate account of current (and much of the past) thinking on the scientific, empirical status of linguistic relativism. We prefer an axis whose end points we will call "minor relativism" and "grand relativism". As opposed, therefore, to a view where either Whorf-like effects hold globally and is inescapable versus has effects so small as to be of no interest, we prefer to think of linguistic relativism as one's language causing various discernible (and measurable) effects on actions/perceptions/beliefs versus one's language being the *cause* of certain large-scale beliefs held by speakers of that language in their descriptions of reality, of how/why their culture works, and their worldview, perhaps accompanied by similarly large differences in behaviour. Of course, being an axis along which there can be variation, we also are open to a number of cases "in the middle"; as well, we think that this axis might be nonincremental so that there are different and not directly comparable ways to be "somewhere along the axis". Results in this "middle area" we call *medial relativism*.

Another distinction—orthogonal to the previous "strong/weak" and "grand/medial/minor" distinctions—is most forcefully brought out in discussions of the emic-etic distinction. Now, the emic-etic distinction can be drawn or explained in many different ways (as a quick perusal of the relevant literature will attest). We like to view it (in the current discussion) as distinguishing between experimentation along the lines we characterized in §4.2—where some linguistic feature of speakers of two languages L_1 and L_2 gives rise to consistently observable behaviour distinction between the two groups of speakers—and cases of less independently observable response in action and instead some overt (but subtle) changes in the attitudes, beliefs, and perhaps even "worldviews" of speakers of L_1 and L_2. While this difference is perhaps not quite the intended distinction between etic and emic investigations (respectively), it does seem to capture an important difference in types of explanation that different researchers in the area employ. And the latter case seems to be more in accord with the initial motivation and types of evidence reported by Whorf (the types of evidence and conclusions he drew that we cited from him in §3.5 and §3.4).

Another path into the etic-emic distinction can be at least partially grasped by analogy with the phon*etic*/phon*emic* distinction. A *phone* is a record of the measurable features (acoustic, normally, but also physiological) of a certain sound, in principle covering all the sounds used in any language, without any account of what systemic uses or patterns occur in various languages. A *phoneme* is the specific set of sounds produced in a specific language, and which is distinguishable by (native) speakers of that language from the other phonemes of that language, and which in turn distinguish different words of the language. In some intuitive sense, phonetics is the study of the physical properties of sounds relevant to languages while phonemics is the study of the mentation involved by speakers of a specific language to group or understand a set of possibly distinct phonemes as being manifestations (or causes) of a particular phoneme. Again, phonetics is a study "from the outside" of sounds of a language, whereas phonemics is the study of how those sounds are interpreted "from the inside" by speakers of a language.

4.4 Minor Relativism

Prime minister of England William Gladstone (1809–1898), who happened also to be a classics scholar, wrote in 1858, concerning his readings of ancient Greek literature,[4] that the only conclusion that could be drawn from these writings is that the ancient Greeks were colour-blind. They could not "see" that (what we call) dark blue shades into (what we call) light blue, and that there are numerous blue-shades

---

[4] In particular, the phrase οἴνοπα πόντον [οἴνοπα = οἶνος (*wine*) + ὄπς (*face or eye*) yields a literal translation as *wine-faced sea*.] The Liddell/Scott/Jones *Greek-English Lexicon* says the phrase is used some 15–20 times in the *Iliad* and *Odyssey*, describing stormy seas. The word οἴνοπα occurs in only one other context in Homer, where it seems to characterize a "dark red".

between the two. He was also exercised by the description of the Aegean Sea as *wine-looking* ... and blood as being coloured *purple*.[5]

We have already mentioned some of the many studies concerning the effect of the sort of colour terms and distinctions one's native language uses on a variety of observable (and etically measurable) actions, including subconscious-level effects. These seem incontravertible evidence of the effects of one's native colour language, although these have so far been shown to be rather minor effects. They also would seem to have minor emic effects in their interaction with one's culture and "Worldview". So we think it apposite to characterize these effects as cases of minor relativity.

A seeming more striking example is the use, in the Australian aboriginal language Guugu Yimithirr (GY), of cardinal directions ("absolute directions") in describing the location of anything, whereas SAE languages make use of "relative directions". English, for example, uses the words/phrases *to the left of, behind, in front of, across, beneath,* ... , whereas GY employs four terms for spatial quadrants: "northern edge, southern edge, eastern edge, western edge". Using examples from (Levinson, 1997, p. 100), when in GY one wishes to describe someone as standing front of a tree, one says (in translation) "George is just north of the tree." To tell someone to take the next left turn, one might say "Go north"; to tell someone to move over a bit "Move a bit east"; and so on. "So thoroughgoing is the use of cardinal directions in GY that, just as we think of a picture as containing virtual space, so that we describe an elephant as behind a tree in a children's book (based on apparent occlusion), so GY speakers think about it as an oriented virtual space: if I am looking at the book while facing north, then the elephant is north of the tree, and if I want you to skip ahead in the book, I'll ask you to go further east (because pages are flipped from east to west)" (Levinson, 1997, p. 100).

The Guugu Yimithirr language is far from unique in this use of cardinal directions, as documented in various works (such as Senft,

---

[5] Actually, he did not believe that they were colour-blind, despite his words from 1858. He later "clarified" that Homer "operated, in the main, upon a quantitative scale ... – light and dark, for its opposite extremities, instead of the qualitative scale opened by the diversities of colour." See Deutscher (2010, pp. 25–45); see also Sampson (2013) for further discussion, sympathetic to "what Gladstone said".

1997, 2007, 2017; Pederson et al., 1998; Haviland, 1998; Haun et al., 2011; Yun and Choi, 2018, for example). These works also cite the fact that, although many of these native speakers of "cardinal direction languages" are bilingual with a "relative direction language" (often, but not always, English), they usually find the employment of relative directions difficult to understand and they usually avoid using them in speech. Most of these authors take this as evidence of conflicts in the speaker's "worldview".

4.5 Medial Relativism

A possibly more "radical" place along the minor–grand axis takes a cue from the many remarks Whorf made concerning how the "relativity of thought" is supposed to be understood: one's language instills habits of thought that influence psychological processes. They do this by having a person *habitually* or *by default* think in certain ways ... ways that she wouldn't habitually have thought had she been raised in a (suitably) different language. Evidence for this type of medial relativism would need to show that the influence manifests itself in nonlinguistic differences of behaviour. This is not a trivial claim, as Whorf, (1941b, pp. 137–138) acknowledged: "the difficulty of appraising such a far-reaching influence is great because of its background character, because of the difficulty of standing aside from our own language, which is a habit and cultural non est disputandum".

One of Whorf's most striking claims concerned the claim that various Amerindian speakers "conceptualized time differently" from SAE speakers. We cited various of these claims in §3.6.2, for instance his view that Hopi have a "fused space/time conceptual scheme where space and time interpenetrate". Various attempts have been made to empirically verify consequences of two languages having different time expressions. Even though Swedish and Spanish are both SAE languages, Bylund and Athanasopoulos (2017) compared Swedish and Spanish speakers on a task to reproduce a duration of a stimulus. The "preferred expressions" of duration differ (Swedish prefers *long–short* while Spanish prefers *much–small*). Swedish-Spanish bilinguals performing the same task in both languages show different interferences, depending on the linguistic context (especially in difficult discriminations); but the difference disappears when the linguistic cues are removed on the same stimuli. The authors conclude that they have revealed "the malleable nature of human time representation" due to the human information processing system.

A different sort of finding is reported in various writings of Lera Boroditsky and colleagues (Boroditsky, 2001; Casasanto et al., 2004; Boroditsky et al., 2011)where it is argued that experimental evidence shows that "Mandarin speakers are more likely than English speakers to make explicit use of the vertical axis when mapping out time". In Mandarin, speakers show evidence of vertical representations of time and talk about time, but English speakers show a strong preference of a left-to-right axis, which follows writing direction. These authors claim that this is predicted by patterns in language, with Mandarin speakers placing earlier time-points above and later time-points below, on the vertical axis. In Boroditsky et al. (2011), the authors say: "the difference between the two groups was predicted by patterns in spatio-temporal metaphor in English and Mandarin. The results provide evidence of a cross-cultural difference in temporal reasoning in an implicit, non-linguistic task. It appears that speakers of different languages automatically activate different culturally-specific spatial representations when reasoning about time" (p. 127).

It should be noted that many of these results have shown resistance to replication. January and Kako (2007) attempt six different replication studies of this particular experiment and find no support for Boroditsky's Whorfian conclusions.

Various positions in some recent and contemporary social movements are strongly committed to this type of indirect support of the concept of linguistic relativism. Certain language reforms have been widely accepted in current (English-speaking) cultures. One that currently passes almost without comment is mentioned in Gentner and Goldin-Meadow (2003, p. 8):

> Terms like *senior citizens, hearing impaired*, and *learning disabled* are assiduously used instead of terms like *old, deaf,* and *dumb*. Interestingly, academicians—even while rejecting the [Whorfian] hypothesis in their work—joined others in our culture in behaving as

though they believed that language could shape thought. Consider the example of *chairman*, now replaced by the term *chair*. . . . Presumably the male-oriented label came about because men were the typical occupants of leadership positions; in this sense, our language reflected the state of the world. But why do we think it so important to change the term now? We seem to believe that calling the position *chairman* potentiates a gender bias, and that calling it *chair* can subtly change our perceptions so that we will be less likely to assume that the position should be filled by a male. Insisting upon the word *chair* seems to reflect a folk belief that changing our language can contribute to changing our cognition. Yet despite embracing . . . this folk belief in their personal behavior, most cognitive researchers continued to find the [Whorfian] language-and-thought hypothesis unworthy of serious consideration in their professional life.

As another perhaps more far-reaching example of this: the feminist critique of language sees current language as a mode of maintaining a patriarchal culture, and follows this critique with a call to "conceptual engineering"—which is a recommendation to change the way we speak so as to effect a change in the underlying concepts. For example,[6] we English speakers[7] denigrate and force the referent of the subject term into patriarchal categories with stereotypic properties when we say *Sally is a female*. Rather, we should say *Sally is female*, using adjectival formulations rather than category terms. If one identifies Sally with a group that she is a member of, then generic, stereotypical properties and features of that group get attributed to Sally. But if Sally is characterized only by mentioning a property that she in fact possesses, such inferences are claimed not to arise. Again, this is linguistic relativism: changing how we talk about a certain group of people we change the way we think about them, changing our individual worldviews and ultimately our culture. In turn, it is alleged, this will bring

---

[6] The following example is from Ritchie (2021b), but authors of very many other works make the same claim about these and related examples of "conceptual engineering". A very nice introduction to, and survey of, current work on conceptual engineering is Isaac et al. (2022).

[7] And presumably all native speakers of languages that distinguish grammatically between a noun (a kind-term) and an adjective that indicates a property had only by that kind.

about a serious change in the behaviour of members of the culture and in the world where these members live. It is more far-reaching than minor relativism in that it (supposedly) will change various habitual social beliefs that are unconsciously caused by the particular ways our current language works. On the other hand, this does not seem to rise to the level of the sort of cases we mention in §4.6.

Similarly, current talk in "socially conscious" news reporting moves even further away from the case of an allegedly offensive noun by eschewing even the relevant adjective, and paraphrasing with a gerundial clause. Consider the shift from *The homeless* ⟼ *Those who are homeless* ⟼ *Those who are experiencing homelessness* ⟼ *The unhoused*. As Gentner and Goldin-Meadow (2003) say, those who do this are obviously under the impression that it will alter the social behaviour (beyond just our words) of members of the society.

The conceptual engineering movement enjoys support not only from a considerable number of current philosophers but also from a number of empirical studies concerning the effects of using generic statements and other types of kind-referring terms. See, for example, Ritchie (2021a); Foster-Hanson et al. (2016); and Sterken (2019), as well as the very many works on the psychological and social effects of "genericity in language", for instance in Rhodes et al. (2012); Wodak et al. (2015); Cimpian and Leslie (2017); Rhodes et al. (2017, 2019); and Leshin et al. (2021), just to pick one dimension of work on the psychology and sociology involved in this topic.

Lera Boroditsky and various coauthors have investigated a number of other, and rather surprising, possible examples of linguistic features being responsible for certain "unexpected" beliefs of speakers of the languages. These are not direct cases of a "testable Whorfian hypothesis" such as those we recounted in §4.2, since they don't explicitly describe nonlinguistic cognitive effects (although the various authors involved in these examples probably think the responses that are elicited could be extended to some nonlinguistic effects). The case that has garnered most attention concerns gender assignments, but not along the lines of the "conceptual engineering" example cited earlier.

It is first established that across languages, speakers of the languages associate the concepts of *male* and *female* with different concepts (from each other) but the same concepts (across the languages); across languages *male* is associated with concepts such as *useful, strong, hard, big, sturdy, dangerous, . . .* ; and *female* is associated with *beautiful, elegant, pretty, slender, peaceful, fragile, ...* Boroditsky et al. (2003) report an experiment involving native German and native Spanish speakers who were also rated very high as fluent speakers of English. Twenty-four terms were chosen that had opposite grammatical gender in German and Spanish: 12 were feminine in German and masculine in Spanish, and 12 were masculine in German and feminine in Spanish. These 24 terms were presented to these subjects in English, and they were asked to write down the first three (English) adjectives that came to mind in describing each object. After collecting these responses, a group of native English speakers, who were unaware of the purpose of the experiment, were asked to evaluate the adjectives as describing masculine or feminine properties. The results were that the German and Spanish subjects *were* influenced by the grammatical gender of the term *in their native language*, even though they were tested in English. And as a whole, all the terms that were grammatically masculine in German (hence feminine in Spanish) were evaluated "in a masculine way" by German speakers and "in a feminine way" by Spanish speakers (and conversely for the opposite grammatical gender terms), even though the test was in English, which has no such grammatical gender assignments. The authors conclude: "these findings once again indicate that people's thinking about objects is influenced by the grammatical genders their native language assigns to the objects' names."

Again, though, researchers have had difficulties with replicating these results. Mickan et al. (2014) conduct two experiments to verify the connection between grammatical gender and stereotypical gender associations in speakers. They fail to replicate any aspect of the original experiment. In fact, it would be quite surprising if indeed these results were true. Different–even contiguous—language families with similar cultures assign grammatical gender to objects in diverse ways. If there were some hidden principle of linguistic cognition, you would expect uniformity in terms of grammatical gender assignment, not the diversity that is usually witnessed within and across similar cultures.

A different realm of investigation is spatial relationship. Korean and English differ in that English divides up spatial relations essentially on the basis of containment (using *in*) and support (using *on*). Korean divides up these relations on the basis of tight-fit versus loose-fit, cutting across the categories of containment and support, and thus giving four basic categories of these sorts of spatial relationship. English on the other hand has just two basic relationships for this type of situation: being-in (containment of any [physical] sort) versus being-on (support of any [physical] type). Yun and Choi (2018) report a large-scale study of monolingual Korean and English speakers (144 subjects in each language, evenly divided between males and females in each language). They were shown video clips of an event and were to verbally describe it in a simple sentence in their native language. The resulting analysis of this large dataset revealed not only substantial overlap between English and Korean speakers on some types of the stimuli but also substantial differences. A "universalist" attitude towards this sort of study ought to predict that since the subjects' sense organs are the same, their language descriptions ought to match. But a "relativistic" viewpoint would instead predict that the linguistic differences should overrule the perceptual descriptions. The authors concluded:

> we have presented empirical data showing a significant convergence between patterns of language-specific spatial semantics and those of nonlinguistic spatial categorization. Detailed analyses of the language data tested against the nonlinguistic data have revealed a complex and intimate relationship between language and spatial perception/cognition. Both systems contribute importantly to language-specific semantic organization as well as to nonlinguistic spatial categorization. The two components influence each other in certain areas but in other areas keep their own functions independent of the other. More specifically, while universal perception/cognition is the foundation to the linguistic system, each language reorganizes the perceptual structure in a specific way for semantic purposes, bringing out certain distinctions to the forefront and collapsing others. Language-specific semantics, in turn, greatly influence the level of perceptual strength particularly of

those features that are malleable in the perceptual system, rendering significant cross-linguistic differences in the relevant nonlinguistic cognitive domain. (p. 1771)

A further avenue of relevant research concerns counterfactual reasoning, where one reasons about consequences of a known- (or believed-) to-be-false supposition, has also been seen as a possible realm for a case of Whorfianism that would be more "striking" than colour-chip differences. Probably this started with Bloom (1981), who used a questionnaire survey and concluded that the Chinese generally found it hard to answer counterfactual questions. But the dispute quickly escalated: a few of the very many responses and counter-responses are Au, (1984a), Bloom (1984), Au (1984b), Cheng (1985), Liu (1985), Wu (1994), Yeh and Gentner (2005), Feng and Yi (2006), Hsu (2013). A recent overview (Jaing, 2019) reviews the linguistic literature and postulates that Chinese has a number of possible ways that a speaker can state (and reason about) counterfactuals but does not commit to any one in particular.

> Jaing's final remark is this: this chapter can be viewed as an exercise in *semantic botany*, which is taken to precede any attempts at formalization and theorization, as it is necessary to establish first some minimal common ground on this much neglected and rather controversial topic in Chinese linguistics. (Jaing, 2019, p. 290)

It seems clear that the jury is out on this topic, despite the fact that the weight of academic opinion is against the Bloom hypothesis. But it certainly would make a good case for a medial Whorfianism, were it to turn out to be correct.

4.6 Grand Relativism

Futuristic political and science fiction literature is a good place to find grand relativism. In Ayn Rand's 1938 novel *Anthem*, a (communist) society is imagined where the very possibility of individualism is eliminated by removing the word "I" from the language. In George

Orwell's 1954 novel *Nineteen Eighty-Four*, the language Newspeak is created and imposed by the State with the intent to constrain and control the thoughts of the speakers. Speakers of this language simply *cannot* think of anti-State sentiments, and this was due to the reduction of number of words in the language with the (supposed) effect of reducing the thought of its speakers. In Samuel Delany's 1966 science fiction novel *Babel-17*, a language is formed with the intent to enhance speakers' analytic abilities and to turn them into more successful political agents. In 1982, Suzette Elgin created the language Láadan, apparently with the dual motives of furthering Neuro-Linguistic training and testing the Sapir-Whorf hypothesis.[8] This language was featured in her 2000 novel *Native Tongue* (as well as two further books in this trilogy), where it was meant to show a more "female-oriented" worldview, as opposed to the SAE worldview, which was considered to be "male-oriented". Max Berry's *Lexicon* (2013) imagined a society of "poets" who had discovered that certain words, when uttered in specific orders, could induce a specific type of listener to be persuaded to believe things (and thereby perform certain actions) that they would not otherwise entertain or do. One character explains: "Persuasion stems from understanding. We compel others by learning who they are and turning it against them." Another remarks "A word is a recipe. A recipe for a particular neurochemical reaction. . . . [We] drop recipes into people's brains to cause a neurochemical reaction that knocks out filters; allowing us to slip an instruction past." Ted Chaing's award-winning novella *Story of Your Life* (1999)—which was adapted for the popular 2016 movie *Arrival*-postulated a space-travelling species whose written language consisted of circles of chains of semantic markers on 2-D surfaces showing no linear (or any other) order. A human linguist managed finally to understand and write in this language. But when she wrote in it, she found her trains of thought became directionless, conclusions and premises could not be distinguished, her sense of the order of time became weak, and many events—both past and future—seemed to become simultaneous.[9] (This appears to be, in the novella, an example

---

[8] See the ongoing work on Láadan, as well as its motivations, at laadanlanguage.com. Unlike the other writers cited in this paragraph, Elgin (1936–2015) was a linguist of some note: see for example Elgin (1972, 1979), among other works.

[9] Sort of a stronger or more forceful version of the Boroditsky work on the direction of time (Boroditsky, 2001) introduced earlier.

of Whorf's analysis of time in Hopi. The movie is more explicit in citing Whorfianism generally.)[10]

These inventions are what we have in mind when talking about "grand relativism". These are the sort of characterizations that excite the imagination of "ordinary citizens"; these sorts of descriptions are the fuel for "the undergraduate disease". On the other hand, these are the sort of imaginative stories that cause relevatist-deniers to accuse the grand relativists of any shred of scientific mentation: "What are the independent and dependent variables in a test/experiment of the claim that features of the language cause those effects? How can these variables be measured?!" And so on...

But as we've said, the minor–grand axis allows for many gradations between the end-points (and as we also said, it allows for many different pathways). So it might therefore be the case that there are "minor" cases that are confirmed, and so a number of related cases of "medial relativism" might become deemed to have clear independent and dependent empirical variables. This could lead to more and more "grand" experiments that also have well-defined measures, approaching the imagined politico/science-fiction scenarios that our novelists have written about... but not quite so outré.

Perhaps cases of idealization in theoretical science might provide an analogy for the methodology suggested in the preceding paragraph. For example, relativistic time dilation is empirically supported by comparing readings of atomic clocks on Earth and on satellites, but satellite velocity is well under 1% of the speed of light. So the empirical evidence supports only a very small segment of a curve, and the rest—which is claimed to be supported by this result—is idealization.[11] Other such examples will probably come to the mind of the reader. A buildup of examples of minor relativism might likewise engender some confidence that medial relativism—or even varieties of grand relativism – must be true in order to have a unified account of the natures of language, culture and worldview, even though the full range hasn't been tested (and maybe is such that it can't be tested, even in theory).

---

[10] For some learned works on science fiction and language/linguistics—often with commentary about Whorf—see for example, Barnes (1975); Meyers (1980).

[11] Thanks to Allen P. Hazen for this example.

5
Linguistic Relativity and Cognitive Science

In this chapter, we evaluate to what extent linguistic relativity (of some form) is integrated into recent and contemporary cognitive science. We interpret cognitive science as broad enough to encompass philosophy, linguistics, psychology, and artificial intelligence (AI). This is an important question given that the concept emanated from work in what would now be considered to be cognitive anthropology, a recent member of an ever-expanding group. In §5.1 we make a case for a certain parallelism between the tripartite structure of linguistic relativity (argued in §5.4) and the structure of the linguistic turn in analytic philosophy, ordinary language philosophy, and contemporary African philosophy. In §5.2, we explore an argument that recreates room for linguistic relativity within modern linguistic theory in spite of the assumed opposition between their foundations. In §5.3, we ask the question whether cognitive linguistics and (4E) approaches to cognition offer a natural place for linguistic relativity to thrive in spite of their movement away from a language centred ontology. Lastly, we close off this chapter with a novel relativity argument based on current natural language processing (NLP) and machine learning applications of large language models in AI.

These discussions serve to highlight the continued presence of linguistic relativity across the cognitive sciences and AI. These are relatively novel observations which showcase the applicability of our analysis of the concept. They also make room for its continued presence and relevance within the scientific community well into the future.

5.1 The Linguistic Turn in Philosophy

It is an open question whether (or how) linguistic relativity is connected to what is called the 'linguistic turn' in analytic philosophy. Part of the reason that this fascinating line of inquiry remains underexplored is the vagueness inherit in both concepts. We have detailed the issues of interpretation which beset linguistic relativity (and Whorfianism). The linguistic turn suffers from a similar set of interpretation problems. From the various writings on the topic, it is unclear whether it was an event, an epoch, or a methodology (or all of the above). We will not attempt any detailed historiography here. Instead, we will follow Williamson (2007) in his approach of treating it at the intuitive level of a "theme" which methodologically informed various philosophers (and other scholars) across analytic philosophy.

The term itself gained initial traction from a volume edited by Richard Rorty in 1967. In it, Rorty claims that "the purpose of the present volume is to provide materials for reflection on the most recent philosophical revolution, that of linguistic philosophy" (Rorty, 1967, p. 3).[1] The basic idea behind the turn draws from many historical antecedents including the Cambridge School of Analysis (Russell and Moore), Frege's logicist programme, and the logical positivism of the early twentieth century. In one way, the linguistic turn can be viewed in a light similar to other 'cleansing' projects over the history of Western philosophy. When metaphysical exuberance infects the field, some figure (be it Kant or Wittgenstein) arrives to reset the agenda and establish some conceptual hygiene for future research.[2] Hacker (2013) argues that it was Wittgenstein in the *Tractatus* who first "took the turn". In fact, Hacker argues that Wittgenstein was the only one to truly do so. However, many adherents of ordinary language philosophy took their inspiration from the later Wittgenstein's thoughts on the relationship between language and philosophy which also bestowed a certain centrality to the analysis of language. However enticing the

---

[1] Rorty himself attributes the term to Bergmann, who uses it to distinguish between two schools of 'linguistic philosophy' (formalist and antiformalist) and establish a middle ground (Bergman, 1952).
[2] Most recently, Ladyman and Ross (2007) set themselves this task of clearing the metaphysical excesses of modern metaphysics in a very similar vein.

task, exegetical details and the fight for the soul of analytic philosophy won't detain us here (see Beaney, 2013, for more on those issues).

Michael Dummett, who firmly links the birth of analytic philosophy to the taking of the linguistic turn (and Frege's legacy), outlines three essential tenets of the turn, and thereby the quiddity of analytic philosophy in general, as: "first, that the goal of philosophy is the analysis of the structure of thought; secondly, that the study of *thought* is to be sharply distinguished from the study of the psychological process of *thinking*; and, finally, that the only proper method for analysing thought consists in the analysis of language" (Dummett, 1978, p. 458).

As Williamson notes, Dummett goes beyond Rorty in taking the turn to be not only methodological principle but a proper subject matter as well. The first and third tenets thus correspond quite closely to linguistic relativity, that is, the only conduit to the structure of thought is via the analysis of human (public) language. However, the second tenet offers some resistance. Most of the versions of linguistic relativity we have explored have explicitly targeted actual thinking processes (whether of colour terms or coordinate systems). In a sense, Dummett uses both 'thought' and 'language' in a way that abstracts over the vicissitudes of individual languages and the possibilities of idiosyncratic thought processes of particular communities. The irrelevance of particular languages is highlighted by Russell's (1905) analysis of proper names as revealing a hidden structure underlying the ambiguity of English surface structure. Taking the 'psychological process of *thinking*' more seriously would move us closer to the cognitive anthropological lens of Sapir and Whorf. Nor is Dummett committed to any directional determinism in terms of the effect of language on cognition. Language is indeed a window into the mind but this does not mean that the structures of language determine the structures of thought. For example, metaphysics is not banished under this conception of philosophy. Rather it is reduced to questions of linguistic analysis.

If anything, Russell, Moore, and Dummett might be committed to *minor relativism*: individual languages could have minor effects on our thinking but the relationship between language and thought transcends these effects. The Wittgenstein of the *Tractatus*, on the other hand, seems to occupy a different position on the relativity spectrum. There, among many other things, Wittgenstein argues that "the sentences of our languages, fully analysed, necessarily reflect the metaphysical form of the world" (Hacker, 2007, p. 8). The picture theory of meaning (or language) entails a constitutive relationship between language and reality. A statement is only meaningful if it provides a picture of reality. If the language of philosophy fails to provide such an image, then it is either beyond language or simply meaningless. The positivists, of course, ran with this idea and used it as a battering ram against speculative metaphysics. Nevertheless, the early Wittgenstein seemed to be exposing something quite close in spirit to *Grand Relativism* in that the bounds of language are used to define the bounds of our reality to some extent, or at least our meaningful talk about that reality.

The early work of Rudolf Carnap and the later work of Donald Davidson highlight the deep connections between these debates in philosophy as well as questions concerning the structure of linguistic relativity. For example, in Davidson (1973) the very concept of radically different conceptual schemes or conceptual packages for viewing the world relies on the possibility of genuine untranslatability. He thinks if such a language existed then we would not be able to consider it to be a language at all (from our perspective). Thus, for him, the fact that we often do describe abstruse foreign concepts in our own languages is testament to their translatability (in principle).[3] Carnap was notoriously sceptical of ordinary languages and even recommended their regimentation for scientific and philosophical purposes. Therefore, his notion of a 'linguistic framework' (or *Aufbau*) differed from Davidson's concept of a language in important respects. But he held on to the idea that conceptual schemes could differ and even be largely incommensurate. For example, in Carnap (1950), he discusses the pragmatics of adopting a framework for abstract entities in science. Inquiring as to the independent existence of such constructs constitute 'external questions' which can receive no serious answer. Thus, we have a possible emic/etic distinction in the language of science. The structure of linguistic frameworks can even perhaps provide a model for linguistic relativity in the natural case despite their nonidentity.

[3] Davidson also held that language and thought were codeterminate of one another.

The linguistic turn, whatever it exactly is or was, places language and its analysis at the centre of the philosophical project.[4] If philosophy is the study of our 'worldviews' (or cognition/thought) to any extent, then this implies that language can play a role (perhaps the only thing that can) in determining the nature of that worldview. The problem is that this thesis doesn't get us to linguistic relativity without an appreciation of the possibility that some languages offer importantly different analyses of reality. Philosophers who held onto the idea of a logical structure underlying natural language that was either imperfectly represented by it or an eventual suitable replacement for it might have taken the linguistic turn. But they were unlikely to have done so via the linguistic relativity on-ramp. As Rorty noted in his description of the turn, "I shall mean by 'linguistic philosophy' the view that philosophical problems are problems which may be solved (or dissolved) either by reforming language, or by understanding more about the language we presently use" (Rorty, 1967, p. 3). The "understanding our language" move is exemplified by both the erstwhile ordinary language philosophy (of the Oxford school) and contemporary analytic African philosophy, while "reforming our language" offers limited connection to relativism of any form.

In the next two subsections, we briefly explore the two movements in analytic philosophy which come closest to connecting the linguistic turn to linguistic relativity, of the medial variety.

5.1.1 The Argument from Ordinary Language

Whorfianism, and by proxy linguistic relativity, is ultimately concerned with the effects natural languages have on cognition, culture, and ontology. Natural languages, on this view, are found in linguistic communities of speakers and signers. Their surface forms can certainly be formally studied in a robust manner. But the kind of linguistic analysis of names given by Russell would surely have been anathema

---

[4] Importantly, as Williamson notes, "but merely to regard linguistic analysis as one philosophical method among many is not yet to have taken the linguistic turn" (Williamson, 2007, p. 10).

to linguists like Whorf.[5] These analyses recommend discarding surface structure in favour of some underlying logical patterning, a move motivated on philosophical and mathematical grounds as opposed to linguistic ones. One previously prominent strand of analytic philosophy, namely ordinary language philosophy, went down a different path.

If the positivists were largely inspired by the early Wittgenstein of the *Tractatus*, the ordinary language philosophers drank from the well of his later work, especially the *Philosophical Investigations* (Wittgenstein, 1953).[6] As Sapir, Whorf, and anthropological linguists studied the structure of ordinary languages spoken by communities of speakers as a reflection of their cultural values and ontological systems, so too did philosophers like Gilbert Ryle and John Austin. For the latter, the way language is actually used by speakers could set the agenda for how philosophy was to precede. Specifically, the idea that certain philosophical claims and theories could receive edification by the analysis of actual linguistic practice of speakers (without logical reconstruction!) is quite radical. In fact, ordinary language use might show us that a particular philosophical problem is a pseudo-problem after all. For example, the knowledge skeptic doubting the existence of the table in front of him merely belies the use of ordinary talk about knowing. Any philosopher's nonstandard or nonordinary use of a term in turn relies on the ordinary usage, which she often distorts for the sake of philosophical argument. As Ryle discusses at length:

> I want to begin by contrasting the phrase 'the use of ordinary language' with the similar-seeming but totally different phrase 'the ordinary use of the expression "...".' When people speak of the use of ordinary language, the word 'ordinary' is in implicit or explicit contrast with 'out-of-the-way', 'esoteric', 'technical', 'poetical', 'notational' or, sometimes, 'archaic'. 'Ordinary' means 'common', 'current', 'colloquial', 'vernacular', 'natural', 'prosaic', 'non-notational', 'on the tongue

---

[5] According to Heijenoort (1967) Russell was a universalist about logic in that he held logic to be an innate interpreted linguistic substrate as opposed to an uninterpreted calculus.

[6] On the (sometimes hostile) relationship between positivism and ordinary language philosophy, see Cavell (1976).

of Everyman', and is usually in contrast with dictions which only a few people know how to use, such as the technical terms or artificial symbolisms of lawyers, theologians, economists, philosophers, cartographers, mathematicians, symbolic logicians and players of Royal Tennis. There is no sharp boundary between 'common' and 'uncommon', 'technical' and 'untechnical' or 'old-fashioned' and 'current'. (Ryle, 1953, p. 167)

In many ways the idea of reading the ontological commitments of speakers off their ordinary linguistic practice is germane to linguistic relativity. In this circumscribed sense, Whorf himself might have been an ordinary language philosopher. But were the ordinary language philosophers Whorfians or relativists? This direction seems more fraught. The major discrepancy came in terms of cross-linguistic methodological rigour or lack thereof on the part of the Oxford philosophers. On this point, Vendler (1971) is especially critical. Vendler focuses on the use of ordinary language analysis in Ryle's infamous attack on Cartesianism in *The Concept of Mind*:

since Ryle's discussion in *The Concept of Mind*, some obviously philosophical conclusions have been drawn from the fact that certain crucial verbs like *know, believe,* or *love,* unlike, say, *run, study,* or *think,* have no continuous tenses. While I can say that I am studying geometry, I cannot say that I am knowing geometry. For this and similar reasons, philosophers have concluded that while studying and the like are actions or processes, knowing and the like are states or dispositions. The trouble, however, is that this distinction cannot be made in German or French—or, indeed, in most of the Indo-germanic languages. And how should one know that other arguments of this kind will hold in languages other than English? What shall we say then? That, for instance, knowing is not a process in English? But what sort of a philosophical thesis is this? (Vendler, 1971, p. 251)

Well, it's a linguistic relativist philosophical thesis. The problem is that the ordinary language philosophers were not trying to make such a claim but rather a universal one about the invariant use of particular concepts. However, without proper attention to cross-linguistic analysis, such claims become dubious, as Vendler goes on to note:

> what we definitely should not do is to say what Ryle does in 'Ordinary Language': 'Hume's question was not about the word "cause"; it was about the use of "cause". It was just as much about the use of "Ursache". For the use of "cause" is the same as the use of "Ursache", though "cause" is not the same word as "Ursache". . . . This is an incredible claim. How does Ryle know, without an exhaustive study of both languages, that the use of *Ursache* is the same as that of *cause*? How, moreover, can two words ever have the same use in two different languages that do not show a one-to-one correlation of morphemes and syntactic structures? Anyway, in so far as Ryle's claim is understandable it is obviously false: the word *cause* is both a noun and a verb. *Ursache*, on the other hand, is never a verb. (Vendler, 1971, p. 252)

Vendler's diagnosis is that it's the (ordinary language) philosopher's ultimate obsession with the a priori that dooms his pursuit of true linguistic philosophy. In our view, the removal of this constraint might have moved the ordinary language philosopher closer to *medial linguistic relativism*, but with it, that position is somewhat out of reach. In the next section, we discuss a more recent view which merges the linguistic turn, ordinary language philosophy, and linguistic relativity from within the emerging work in the Global South, namely *conceptual decolonization*.

5.1.2 Decoloniality and Wiredu's Tongue Dependence

Universality and hegemony have never been too far from one another in the history of the world. The Oxford philosophers, like many in the West, stopped their analysis at English or at most a limited set of other SAE languages. Whorf's call, if anything, was one towards the theoretical and philosophical fecundity of moving beyond this barrier. In this way, it would not be too far a leap to locate his work within the emerging decolonial literature of the Global South. In fact, decolonial theory itself, although often linked to the Continental tradition in philosophy, is committed to linguistic relativity across our continuum. One particularly controversial exposition of the fundamental difference between the African worldview and the alleged Western one is provided by Placide Tempels in his tendentious *Bantu Philosophy*. In it, he claims Africans or "Bantu have their own ontologies" (Tempels, 1969, p. 99), "their own psychology" (p. 74). He does so without scientific investigation or experimentation; nevertheless he goes on to state: "the metaphysics of Christian thought . . . has been based on a rather static fundamental concept of being. This is where the fundamental difference between Western thought and that of the Bantu and primitives appears. . . . We have a static concept of being, they have a dynamic notion" (p. 32).

Many African philosophers have reacted to this work with indignation. While Tempels might have attempted to present a case for the systematic thought and philosophical acumen of Africans against the then-detractors, he overgeneralized and ultimately adopted many of the racist tropes associated with people of colour at the time (Matolino, 2011). Nevertheless, prominent movements on the continent have argued for the uniqueness of African thought and a distinctive worldview, including Leopold Senghor's celebrated concept of 'Negritude' and the recent work on Ubuntu philosophy in Southern Africa (Metz, 2011). Very often, these claims are grounded in linguistic practice and specific grammatical features of African languages. We won't focus on the grand claims here as they are generally more controversial. Rather we will outline a particular account of 'conceptual decolonisation' proffered by the African analytic philosopher Kwasi Wiredu. Wiredu's account is a blend of *medial relativism* and ordinary language philosophy. His overarching idea is to make room for both universal and particular elements of philosophical cultures (or worldviews) via the comparative analysis of individual (African) languages. In this way he improves upon the limitations of ordinary language philosophy. As a test case, Wiredu (1985) considers the correspondence theory of truth in his native Akan language. He starts in the following way: "ask any ordinary Akan who speaks English what the Akan word for truth is, and unless he/she has made a special study of the matter, the chances are that the answer will be *nokware*. In a certain sense this would be right. A little reflection, however, discloses a complication. The opposite of *nokware* is *nkontompo* which means lies. But the opposite of truth is falsity, not lies" (Wiredu, 1985, p. 234).

He goes on to show that Akan, unlike English, does not have a truth predicate but only the word *saa* ("so") and *te saa* ("is so"). Furthermore, Akan does not contain an equivalent of the word 'fact'. He suggests no idea of expressive incompleteness of Akan on this score. Everything that can be expressed with the English word 'fact' can in fact be said within the associated locution of Akan. Here comes the interesting bit:

> these linguistic contrasts have some very interesting consequences for the theory of truth. Consider the correspondence theory of truth. This is supposed to assert something like this: "p is true" means "p corresponds to a fact". What does this come to in Akan? Simply that "p te saa", which in truth is nothing more than saying that "p saa" means "p te saa". In other words, the correspondence definition amounts to a tautology in Akan. In a certain sense, this might be taken as a verification of the correspondence theory, for it might be said that being a tautology is an especially splendid way of being true. Be that as it may, one thing that cannot be pretended in Akan is that the correspondence theory offers any enlightenment about the notion of being so. (Wiredu, 1985, p. 236)

This shows that some philosophical concepts or insights, such as Tarskian truth, are not universal, according to Wiredu. To the speaker of Akan, his worldview already possesses a correspondence concept. In fact, the concept cannot be formulated in Akan. To see how this argument amounts to a claim about decolonisation, consider the procedure it implies. In order to investigate the profundity of a particular philosophical concept, say one inherited from the Western canon, we first need to filter it through the constructions of our native (non-SAE) languages. There may indeed be universal philosophical concepts on this view but it is an empirical matter as to what they are. Most philosophical problems and theories are thus *tongue dependent*.

What makes Wiredu a medial relativist is that he does not preclude the possibility of universal philosophical concepts shared by all humans. Moreover, he does not suggest that the worldviews embodied in African languages are incommensurate with Western ones in any way. Akan merely encodes a more moral, and less logical, concept of truth according to Wiredu.[7]

In this section, we have traced different versions of linguistic relativism through the twentieth-century history of analytic philosophy. We have shown that the origins of analytic philosophy flirted with the concept while never truly embracing it. We concluded by considering an emerging trend in the analytic philosophy of the Global South that shares features with the linguistic turn and linguistic relativity.

5.2 Linguistics and Relativity

If analytic philosophers of the early to mid-twentieth century were largely unaware of cultural anthropology, their formal linguistic counterparts certainly were. The Chomskyan revolution of that time privileged the theory of a universal substrate common to all human languages. The methodology was more mathematical and less anthropological, thus resulting in less focus on the documentation and preservation of rare non-SAE languages. Under some interpretations, linguistics around the middle of the twentieth century was shifting away from an empiricist grounding and towards rationalist approaches. If the formal study of English could reveal aspects of a universal grammar, then perhaps it was less necessary for linguists to spend their time and efforts on exploring the possible divergences of other less known languages (and families). Emmon Bach was acutely aware of the danger universalism brings with it when he stated in his 1996 presidential address to the Linguistic Society of America: "we need to cherish and study linguistic diversity for reasons that are as important scientifically as they are politically and ethically. It is not a

---

[7] There is some dispute about his linguistic analysis, and oddly enough he denied any commitment to Whorfianism or linguistic relativity. However, he clearly only considered the Grand Relativity version.

bad idea to let a language unfold itself to you on its own terms for a good long while before you jump to fitting it into your theory or testing your theories against it" (Bach, 1996).

In the next section, we mount a controversial argument that generative grammar is actually compatible with linguistic relativity in two interesting ways. In fact, it is compatible with the strongest version on our spectrum, namely *Grand Relativism*. We will first make the standard case for the anti-Whorfian stance of Chomskyan linguistics, and then suggest that there might still be room for linguistic relativity. Lastly, we will discuss recent claims by typologists as to the vast diversity of linguistic categorisation across languages and what this might mean for relativity.

5.2.1 Universal Grammar and Linguistic Diversity

We have mentioned Chomskyan linguistics or the universalist tendency in modern linguistics before. We'll provide a brief overview here before moving on to the rather surprising argument for relativity within generative linguistics.

The key idea behind the rise of generative grammar is that the core structures of natural languages are internal to the 'cognisers' of that language. Philosophers and anthropologists alike have assumed that the public, external symbols which characterize the communicative behaviour of language users (within linguistic communities) constitute the subject matter of linguistics, that is, what a language is. Chomsky and his followers challenged this idea. Their main issue with it was that such a view of language (sometimes called 'E-language') is a scientific nonstarter. Linguistic relativity restated then amounts to the claim that E-languages shape thought or cognition (along the spectrum we proposed). In his discussion of Donald Davidson's quixotic article on malapropisms and the nonexistence of language,[8] Chomsky (2000, p. 70) says the following: "the proper conclusion is not that we must abandon concepts of language that can be productively studied, but that the topic of successful communication in the actual

---

[8] Davidson (1986).

world of experience is far too complex and obscure to merit attention in empirical inquiry, except as a guide to intuitions as we pursue research designed to lead to some understanding of the real world, communication included."

The accusation is that philosophers of language (and those studying E-languages) are doomed to search in vain for a "theory of everything" which will likely only lead them to the discovery of nothing. So if the study of observable patterns of linguistic behaviour does not lead us to the proper subject matter of linguistics, then what does? The answer is in the brain, or rather the more abstracted object 'the mind'. The 'language faculty' is the cognitively isolated or modular seat of language (read: syntax) production and comprehension. Basically, you have a generative grammar in your brain somewhere, which is responsible for structuring the grammatical sentences of your language. What's more, this language faculty is common to all human beings! It is a 'universal' grammar of sorts. "In these terms, we can develop a concept of "knowledge of language" that is appropriate for the inquiry into language and mind; namely, mastery and internal representation of a specific I-language. The linguist's grammar is a theory of the I-language, and universal grammar is the theory of the initial state of the language faculty. Jones's I-language is one particular mature state or output, regarding the language faculty as a function that maps evidence into I-language" (Chomsky, 2000, p. 73).

There's a lot to unpack here.[9] But the important bits for our purposes concern the notion of an 'I-language' or an internalized representation of one's language faculty's mature state (the state attained after language acquisition) and the universal grammar which is the state one starts with. During the heyday of the *principles and parameters* (P&P) framework, there was a very useful analogy with a switchboard. The P&P framework starts with the assumption that we are biologically endowed with a language faculty. This faculty is prewired with two kinds of linguistic features: principles and parametrized principles, or parameters for short. The principles are all fixed and universal

---

[9] This isn't really the place for that. For an overview of the philosophy of linguistics, see Nefdt (2024).

whereas the parameters are like binary switches set at either 'on' or 'off'. The initial state of the system or UG sets all the parameters to off. This is the state into which we are born as children. Then, as we are exposed to more linguistic input from our environments (or primary linguistic data; PLD), the parameters of the language faculty begin to be set to either of the binary options. Once all of the parameters have been set (are turned on or remain off) the faculty of language reaches a steady state.

Linguistic relativity restated within the P&P model implies that the individual switches can alter the universal principles (your UG). But on the generative linguistic picture, this move is strictly vetoed. The standard reason for the veto involves language acquisition and the idea of poverty of stimulus. In a nutshell, children are just not exposed to enough data from the PLD to explain their mastery of the vast structures of human language, which they acquire with alarming alacrity.[10]

Linguistic universalism seems to be directly opposed to relativity. This is the standard bifurcation at least, and a reasonable one at that. But there are two ways out of this consequence, as we see it. One implies a *grand* yet trivial relativism while the other preys on a particular feature of the tenets of generative grammar (thankfully one that has not changed much over the many versions of the theory). Let's start with the surprising one. How on earth does UG and Chomskyan linguistics imply or allow for the possibility that languages might indeed shape cognition? The idea is brought out nicely by a fanciful thought experiment Chomsky often uses to present UG. "On these simplifying assumptions about development, we look just at the cognitive system of the language faculty, its initial state, and its later states. Plainly, there are state changes that reflect experience: English is not Swahili, at least, not quite. A rational Martian scientist would probably find the variation rather superficial, concluding that there is one human language with minor variants" (Chomsky, 2000, p. 118).

---

[10] The slightly more sophisticated version of this claim has it that there are certain kinds of evidence (usually negative evidence) with which they are not supplied. Yet they allegedly systematically avoid certain kinds of errors. See Pullum and Scholz (2002) for a critique.

The Martian linguist looks at the diversity of human languages and sees but one language underlying it: UG. The variations and variety are epiphenomenal effects of the E-language parameters. How can this be? Well, according to Chomsky the proper subject matters of linguistics are I-languages. These are parametrized versions of the same underlying universal language. But if the Martian fails to appreciate much of this nuance, it might be because he has a different UG (or some other mechanism for appreciating UG, maybe an artificial neural network or something; we'll return to this idea in §5.4). This leaves room for the situation in which our UG shapes the way we see the world, as involving thousands of languages. Relativity is at the level of UG. The Martians might have a different UG, and thus 'worldview', and thus might not be able to interact with our I-languages (while our E-language variance would be meaningless). Now we have an interesting explanation of *Arrival*, in which the Heptopods' cognition (and anyone who can translate it) stems from an alternative appreciation of reality. Although grand, this reconstruction of UG is also potentially trivial. Without the aliens, the relativity evaporates, while retaining some remnants in the realm of future close encounters or science fiction.[11]

The more mundane escape hatch, or room for relativity, presents itself in terms of the modularity thesis of generative linguistics. The idea is that the I-language is domain-specific. In the parlance of cognitive science, it is a cognitively impenetrable module detached from general cognition. This means that language does not interact, in causal or constitutive ways, with other parts of our cognition, like planning, perception, and so on. It doesn't mean that perception, planning, or even semantics aren't connected in some ways to language. In a now contentious hypothesis published in the journal *Science*, Hauser et al. (2002) floated the idea of two distinct concepts of the language faculty. One is narrow and basically just contains recursion or syntax. The other involves semantics, pragmatics, and communicative functions. The former is core, the latter peripheral. I-languages presumably live in the core. "All approaches agree that a core property of FLN is recursion, attributed to narrow syntax in the conception.... This capacity

---

[11] Again, we will return to a similar idea that linguistic aliens might already live among us in § 5.4.

of FLN yields discrete infinity (a property that also characterizes the natural numbers)" (Hauser et al., 2002, p. 1571).

To be slightly more specific: the faculty of language in the narrow sense (FLN) contains only syntax or recursion. The faculty of language in the broad sense (FLB) contains this latter component and its interfaces with the sensory-motor and conceptual-intentional systems, for example, phonology and semantics (or maybe better pragmatics since Chomskyans are internalist about semantics). Nothing in this picture precludes the possibility that the FLB affects or constrains cognition. In fact, the FLB is a card-carrying member of the general cognition club. The recluse is FLN. This opens the door for minor to medial relativism. It just requires a slight change in vocabulary. It's not the narrow FLN that shapes cognition but rather the broader FLB that does. Since the FLB is a bona fide linguistic system (the older one, according to Hauser et al., 2002), we still can get 'linguistic' relativity in a broad sense. The thesis just becomes one about the effects that non-'narrow' or nonsyntactic parts of language have on cognition. One consequence of the overarching view is brought out nicely by Berwick and Chomsky in their book on the evolution of FLN: "the appearance of complexity and diversity in a scientific field quite often simply reflects a lack of deeper understanding, a very familiar phenomenon" (Berwick and Chomsky, 2016, p. 93).

Of course, many linguists do not subscribe to this particular picture of the division of linguistic and general cognition. We'll meet some of them in §5.3. For now, we want to preheat the oven by considering a kind of methodological Whorfianism not uncommon within a typology setting.

5.2.2 Typology and Diversity

The natural question to ask about universalism is, of course, where are the universals? Where are these patterns and structures common to all natural languages that the Martians can see? Some linguists have suggested properties or mechanisms like recursion, whether or not actual languages display these properties on the surface. Typologists are less persuaded by deep universals like recursion or syntactic constituency.

They prefer surface forms over theoretical entities. After all, the job description requires the analysis and documentation of the features of the world's languages. So saying that a language possesses a universal property, even if that language doesn't use it, doesn't pay the bills.

It's also curious that prominent typologists have largely resisted the universalism of (generative) theoretical linguistics. Do they know something we don't? Here's a clue as to some of their ruminations on the subject. Evans and Levinson (2009) start their account in the following bold manner:

> languages are much more diverse in structure than cognitive scientists generally appreciate. A widespread assumption among cognitive scientists, growing out of the generative tradition in linguistics, is that all languages are English-like but with different sound systems and vocabularies. The true picture is very different: languages differ so fundamentally from one another at every level of description (sound, grammar, lexicon, meaning) that it is very hard to find any single structural property they share.... Structural differences should instead be accepted for what they are, and integrated into a new approach to language and cognition that places diversity at centre stage. (p. 429)

A genuine appreciation of linguistic diversity seems to be at the heart of both Sapir's and Whorf's writings. What would language studies look like if we approached it from an anti-universalism direction? And moreover, would such an approach lead to something akin to the revival of linguistic relativity?

Interestingly, typologists seem to favour a 'methodological relativity' without necessarily endorsing a cognitive or ontological one. Martin Haspelmath, for instance, has repeatedly distinguished between description of language and comparisons of languages. The latter he suggests, based on cross-linguistic studies, leads to sui generis categories, while the former often enforces some perspectival unification. In Haspelmath (2019), he identifies what he calls the 'Mendeleyevian vision of grammar' in which all grammars are made from the same building blocks, which seems to be a particular precisification of UG.[12] He strongly contests this approach as a mechanism for cross-linguistic comparison, as different languages encode grammatical properties differently. The basic idea is that universalists seem to mine individual languages deeper and deeper to unearth abstract properties of language simpliciter. This, however, skirts over genuine differences in linguistic categorisation. For example, we might try to define a 'grammatical Subject' in such an abstract manner as maybe some syntactic element that imposes agreement on the main verb. But some languages, for example Malagasy, do not follow this pattern. Haspelmath worries that "this procedure is unlikely to pick out uniform phenomena across languages if different subjects may be recognized by different criteria, so how do we know that they are all subjects in the same sense?" (2019, p. 116).

William Croft goes one step further to claim: "across languages as well, constructions appear to define different categories (Dryer 1997): AbsolutiveErgative does not match SubjectObject; the Verb category can be either more inclusive (including 'Adjectives as well) or less inclusive (where a small set of 'Verbs combines with other elements to produce the translation equivalents of English Verbs)" (2013, p. 215).

Croft proposes a radical form of cognitive linguistics called 'radical construction grammar' to counter the building block or universalist view. The typological cry seems to be 'Respect the diversity of structures across languages!' This reminds us of a joke told by Geoff Pullum at a keynote address a few years ago in Scotland: the Martian linguist returning home with news of one human language on Planet Earth is unlikely to receive tenure.

In John McWhorter's book on Whorfianism (2014), the rejuvenated interest in linguistic relativity is located in a noble, antihegemonic pursuit or appreciation of the diversity of world languages and cultures. It is inspired by an urge to both preserve worldviews and decentralize language studies (similar to the decolonial movement we discussed in §5.1.2). The kind of typological analysis Haspelmath and other typologists present conforms to this ideal. However, it does not go further to endorse any explicit form of linguistic relativity

---

[12] Modelled on the success of the periodic table in chemistry.

beyond perhaps the *minor* variety we have described earlier. The fact that languages might encode grammatical concepts distinctly does not entail that those languages also encode distinct worldviews or that they cannot fruitfully be compared and contrasted. The minimum requirement for the further move is a story about how this typological diversity might map onto alternative cognitive expression. In the next sections, we explore the linguistic relativist possibilities presented in cognitive linguistics and the overarching 4E framework in cognitive science more broadly.

5.3 A Return to Cognition

There are a number of core tenets of generative linguistics that militate against the general linguistic relativist picture. Three specific abstractions do most of the work. The first is the identification of language with linguistic competence as opposed to performance. The second is the idea that this competence or the (narrow) language faculty is an innate cognitively isolated module in that it operates independently of general cognition, also called "domain-specific" in the literature.[13] The last is that the mind is a lot like a computer in that it is a manipulator of discrete symbols. This view, known as the computational theory of mind or CTM for short, was part of a larger revolution in cognitive science in the mid-twentieth century led by Chomsky, Fodor, and others.

In this section, we question whether linguistic relativity might fare better within a framework (or family of frameworks) which rejects some or all of these tenets. In §5.3.1, we remove the competence-performance distinction and the modularity thesis. In §5.3, we go a

---

[13] The idea is that the language faculty is like an organ. Of course, the heart relies on the brain and the liver on the gall bladder but they all have their separate functions. Boeckx describes it this way:

> UG has been studied in a modular fashion, as a mental organ, a coherent whole that can be studied in relative isolation from other domains of the mind/brain. Indeed, studies of various pathological cases have shown this mental organ to be biologically isolatable (Boeckx, 2005, p. 46).

step further to consider alternatives to CTM in which the whole body, environment, and even society might be included in cognition.

In a way, we are attempting a reverse of the previous sections. Universalism in linguistics is naturally pitted against relativity. We showed that there might be room for compatibilism nonetheless. Here, one might expect that alternative, and especially dynamic, frameworks in cognitive science might provide a better home for relativity. Oddly enough, we suggest that appearances might be misleading on this score.

5.3.1 Lakoff and the Cognitive Commitment

Let us start with what George Lakoff calls the 'cognitive commitment' or the commitment to "make one's account of human language accord with what is generally known about the mind and brain from disciplines other than linguistics" (1991, p. 54). This injunction doesn't immediately mean that language isn't special, it just confronts the assumption that language is unique or special at the outset. However, in reality this move suggests domain generality or an antimodularity thesis. In making it, the field quickly brought forth the so-called Second Cognitive Revolution, in which language lost its privileged place in the cognitive scientific centre and was replaced by cognitive psychology (initially on the bench due to its overt behaviorist leanings; Sinha, 2012). At least this is how the standard story goes . . .

You might already be worried that linguistic relativity requires some remnant of the idea that language is cognitively special in some way to get off the ground. After all, individual languages are supposed to be windows into cognition and determine distinct worldviews, according to linguistic relativity. Given the hallowed role language played in the classical cognitive revolution, this makes generative linguistics a surprising ally. Furthermore, cognitive linguistics differs from generative linguistics in a number of significant ways. For example, most cognitive linguists reject the autonomy of syntax and consider language to be inextricably semantic. Semantic relativity, or the idea that individual linguistic communities carve up meaning in distinct ways, is a bold claim, on the road to *Grand Relativism*. In fact, it might go against a prominent universalist principle in semantics attributed to Jerrold Katz. Katz's 'effability principle' states that all languages can express every human thought. Given the relatively rapid evolution of human language, this egalitarian principle seems quite plausible, that is, there just hasn't been enough time or separation between human linguistic communities to warrant such expressive departures. Thus, no proposition or meaning is inaccessible to any language. This idea is, of course, directly opposed to *Grand Relativism* (but might still allow for other forms).

But let's not get ahead of ourselves. Cognitive linguistics, unlike some forms of generative linguistics, pairs well with typology and linguistic diversity generally. This is the case because it doesn't carry with it the assumption of a unique language faculty or universal grammar common to all languages. Of course, some aspects of language are likely to be innate, for example, certain default structural biases, but we generally learn our languages from the linguistic communities into which we are born, including syntax! Take construction grammar. In this framework, the building block model of meaning in which meaningful parts are combined to produce meaningful wholes, or what is known as 'compositionality', is rejected (Goldberg, 2015). Compositionality is a mainstay of syntax and semantics from the formalist camp. Their suggested alternative model is one in which language specific 'constructions' play a larger role in both syntax and semantics. Constructions are usually taken to be pairings of form and meaning such that there are slots for saturation, as in "X takes Y for granted". Constructions can range from frozen idiomatic phrases to more flexible and abstract rule-like patterns. For example, to "pull strings" can be modified to "pull X strings" for particular adjectives, such as *academic*, *legal*, or *questionable*. Less flexible constructions, like idioms, are often considered to be untranslatable by particular communities. Construction grammarians claim that these kinds of structures are much more prevalent in natural languages than the combinatoric atomic particles assumed in much of mainstream universalist linguistics.

Let's consider one surprising discovery attributed to cognitive linguistics that seems not only to have opened the door for some sort of relativity but also to have implicitly inspired a number of experiments on the subject. Formal semantics, the mathematical study of the meaning, has mostly focused on literal meaning, that is, the meaning contributed by each subexpression to the meaning of whole expressions, for example, a sentence. This is partly because declarative sentences work well with truth conditional analysis. It's easy to link the meaning of the sentence *The cat is on the mat* with the conditions under which is it true. But we use language in lots of nonliteral ways. We can be sarcastic, poetic, interrogatory, obfuscatory, and so on. The standard approach for a long time has been to treat these kinds of phenomena as parasitic on literalness. A more charitable gloss is that these phenomena are interesting but not from a semantic point of view. Rather, they fall within the realm of pragmatics.[14]

However, Lakoff and Johnson (1980) showed quite convincingly just how pervasive metaphorical language is in human society. Metaphors can shape the way we think about events, abstract objects, and kinds in such a way that they influence (or direct) our actions. Take the case of arguments. Reasons are indefensible, critiques hit their targets, we focus on weak points, and so on. We aim to win them at all costs. This kind of metaphor shapes how we experience arguments and how we act when we are pursuing them. Consider a language in which arguments are linked to dances, or to contracts, or to joint authorship, or . . . instead of wars. This shift in metaphorical colouring might occasion thoughts of collaboration or mutual benefit as opposed to triumph and victory.

According to Lakoff and Johnson (1980), this isn't an isolated phenomenon. Metaphors are ubiquitous. Their power to shape thoughts is unassailable. By using one concept (or object) to understand or experience another, they can reveal conceptual components while hiding other aspects.

---

[14] Bar Hillel (1971) is credited with describing pragmatics as the "waste-basket of linguistics": whatever one cannot explain in syntax and semantics gets moved to the pragmatics folder on the desktop.

Our ordinary conceptual system, in terms of which we both think and act, is fundamentally metaphorical in nature. (p. 3)

New metaphors are capable of creating new understandings and, therefore, new realities. This should be obvious in the case of poetic metaphor, where language is the medium through which new conceptual metaphors are created. (p. 139)

The heart of metaphor is inference. Conceptual metaphor allows inferences in sensory-motor domains (e.g., domains of space and objects) to be used to draw inferences about other domains (e.g., domains of subjective judgment, with concepts like intimacy, emotions, justice, and so on). Because we reason in terms of metaphor, the metaphors we use determine a great deal about how we live our lives. (p. 244)

It is as though the ability to comprehend experience through metaphor were a sense, like seeing or touching or hearing, with metaphors providing the only ways to perceive and experience much of the world. (p. 239)

With these ideas in mind, we can construct an argument for medial linguistic relativism. Languages encode the metaphorical nature of thought processes which shape our quotidian experiences. These metaphors, essentially linguistic expressions frame "understanding and experiencing one kind of thing in terms of another" are language specific (Lakoff and Johnson 1980, p. 5). In English, time is organized in terms of forward-facing future and a backward-facing past. The aptly named tense logician Arthur Prior even mounted a famous critique of the tenseless view of time (favoured by scientifically-minded philosophers) based on the claim that when we think "Thank goodness that's over" after a particularly painful dental surgery, the content of our utterance cannot be grounded in a date or a statement of simultaneity (which tenseless views require). Our thoughts are tensed. Similarly, our thoughts about times in English are based on a linear framework: either a horizontal (and left-to-right, it is usually claimed) metaphor or a behind-to-in-front metaphor. In Mandarin, as Neo-Whorfians have claimed, time moves vertically. The future is above you and the past below. You look up at the future, not forward to it. (However, we remind readers that in §4.5 we mentioned the difficulties many other researchers have had in trying to replicate their experiments.)

If the metaphors which shape our thoughts are language specific, then the experience which those metaphors condition in our communities are equally language specific. The reason this doesn't amount to full-blown or grand relativism is that nothing suggests that these metaphors cannot be intertranslatable or are somehow incommensurable. Mandarin speakers learn English with its horizontal time and English speakers learn Mandarin with its vertical temporality. We can unlearn our militant talk of arguments and embrace more cooperative metaphors with enough therapy.

Furthermore, Lakoff and Johnson (1980, p. 20) insist that metaphors go beyond language or rather are "not just a matter of language, that is, of mere words". Instead they contend that "human thought processes are largely metaphorical" in themselves. This move makes room for us to recognize the ways culture and environment play an important 'world-shaping' role as well. Conceptual metaphors, the crux of Lakoff and Johnson's account, are ways of understanding a target concept in terms of another conceptual domain. One could understand emotional states of people in terms of temperature: angry is hot, depressed is cold, and so on. It's a bit like a measurement theory of mind (since you can map the scale of the one domain onto the other). This process is mediated by language but not bound by it. Pictures or diagrams can also serve as conceptual metaphors. Nevertheless, metaphors can act as framing tools and thus create default or habitual cognitive niches in particular linguistic communities as per medial relativism. What remains to be shown is that alternative approaches to cognition might expand on these possibilities.

5.3.2 4E Approaches to Cognition

If the mind is like a computer, then the brain is often considered to be the hardware on which it runs its programmes. Locating the mind, and by extension the language faculty, in the head implies that linguistic cognition is mostly determined by neurological factors. Given that humans share these intracranial features, universalism again becomes an inviting option. Linguistic philosophy and the analytic tradition in philosophy itself too has been accused of disembodied propositionalism. "In the 70 or so years since the emergence of the field of philosophy of language, there has been remarkably little variance from these early ideas that (1) language is conceptual and propositional, and (2) concepts, propositions, and thoughts are not profoundly shaped by the nature of our bodily capacities and modes of engagement with our material environments, other than as a medium for supplying the content of perceptions" (Johnson, 2018, p. 627).

Cognitive linguistics has an entirely different take on cognition. Instead of embracing internalism about language (and the mind), or disregarding the role the body plays in mental computations, it is usually coupled with one of the *E*s in the 4E approach to cognition, especially *E*mbodied cognition. What could this change in perspective bring to the linguistic relativity debate?

We won't go into too much detail about what each *E* means here (see Dove, 2022). The central idea is that each *E* extends the mind to a different set of modalities. For example, the *E*xtended mind hypothesis (Clark and Chalmers, 1998) suggests that in the way a blind person's walking stick extends or supplements their visual perception, individual cognisers can be coupled with objects in the environment, such as calculators, GPS, perhaps even ChatGPT, to outsource their cognitive processes. Embedded or situated cognition emphasises the role played by the embedding context of thought. Essentially, it reminds us that the separation between a cognitive process, like counting, and the environment which instantiates it, cannot be nonarbitrarily achieved. Once a cognitive practice becomes significantly incorporated or rote, then it can become embedded or internal. Thus, language might be interactive and communicative in nature, but once this process has been internalised it can manifest as inner monologue in the mind of the user. The two *E*s we'll focus on here for an argument towards relativity are *E*mbodied and *E*nactive. Again, Johnson and Lakoff (2002, p. 245) describe the relationship between cognitive linguistics and embodied cognition this way:

what we saw, especially in light of sweeping, rapid developments in cognitive neuroscience, was that meaning is grounded in our sensorimotor experience and that this embodied meaning was extended, via imaginative mechanisms such as conceptual metaphor, metonymy, radial categories, and various forms of conceptual blending, to shape abstract conceptualization and reasoning. What the empirical evidence suggests to us is that an embodied account of syntax, semantics, pragmatics, and value is absolutely necessary for an adequate understanding of human cognition and language. You cannot simply peel off a theory of conceptual metaphor from its grounding in embodied meaning and thought. You cannot give an adequate account of conceptual metaphor and other imaginative structures of understanding without recognizing some form of embodied realism.

What is embodied realism? It's a thesis about meaning in the mind. It states that the essence of experience, meaning, and thought is given by the continuous series of embodied organism–environment interactions. These interactions form the basis for cognition without a separation between mind and body. The doctrine is more empiricist than rationalist in this way. Thus, there is no mind-body dualism but only embodied actions which constitute our understanding of the world. A nice illustration of this idea is given in comparison with nonhuman animal cognition. Peter Godfrey-Smith, among others, has brought the truly amazing structure of the octopus to public attention. The complex behaviour of these molluscs includes camouflage, puzzle solving, jar opening, intricate prey trapping, and so much more. Their bodies are made up of tentacles which act autonomously like little brains. The neural circuitry is patently embodied. According to embodied realism, an octopus's cognition is unlikely to reside somewhere in its cranium. Their embodiment determines their particular brand of cognition, as does ours. Different kinds of bodies, in different kinds of animals, affect or constrain the kinds of cognition an animal can exhibit. Thomas Nagel once pondered what it is like to be a bat. According to this suite of views, it is not only the bat's different brain structure that makes its cognition inaccessible to us but also its body structure. So let's start by acknowledging that the particular embodied interactions we share within our linguistic communities is dependent on the kinds of creatures we are physically.[15]

Next, let us consider what 'enactive cognition' adds to this picture. Basically, enactivism claims that we are not passive participants in the worldview game. From this relatively benign claim, adherents of this view often leap to the idea that humans 'co-create their world' to a large extent. The strength of this idea varies from an implausible phenomenological or Heideggerian interpretation in which we literally actively project the world in front of us, to a more reasonable niche construction account of evolutionary theory.

What does understanding language in terms of embodiment and enactiveness do for linguistic relativity? Let's take the first prong, embodiment. If meaning is derived from complex interactions between our bodily actions and the environment (including other speakers), then somehow those interactions determine or at least influence our cognition. Different communities would require different kinds of interactions to be realised. The language of Inuit communities might then determine different conceptual modalities from those of urban city dwellers in a metropolis. The isolated village setting of the Pirahã might constrain their language to the environmental exigencies and not much else. Outlandish-sounding claims as to the lack of a counting or number system of these groups of people might in turn be lent more credence.

Enactivism adds more ontological enhancement. The cognitively constraining embodied interactions of linguistic communities quite literally cocreate distinct worldviews. This E motivates the position that cognition arises from the active exercise of our sensory-motor actions. In this way we create our own meaning in accordance with the particular kinds of actions our particular kinds of bodies produce. We, like some other animals to different degrees, are 'meaning-makers'. But are we also linguistic relativists?

Here things get tricky. As mentioned at the beginning of this section, cognitive linguistics does not put language at the centre of cognition.

---

[15] Interestingly, the experimental side of the embodied cognition literature has been recently challenged in terms of replication studies, as have the Neo-Whorfian experiments mentioned earlier. See Machery (2024) for more.

Language is just one particular modality. In the same way, when we enact or create worldviews, this process cannot be reduced to some simple causal arrow between language and cognition. Language, as action, is part of a larger cognitive process of meaning creation in the world. In this way, a thesis which states that it is language that separates communities in terms of cognition is not automatically a friendly amendment to 4E cognition or cognitive linguistics. If relativity is endorsed by these views in some way, then said relativity would go beyond language to cultural, environmental, and cognitive possibilities.[16]

In the TV series *Battlestar Galatica,* Earth is destroyed by humanoid cyborgs (called Cylons). Humans are forced to leave the planet and float around on one of the last remaining spaceships while avoiding their extinction at the hands of the Cylons, who occupy outer space. This new environment and set of circumstances, according to embodied and enacted cognition, will inevitably alter human cognition. We will have to make new worldviews and new meanings, some of which are represented in the show. Language will certainly help us achieve this goal but it won't determine the worldview we eventually cohabit.

What we have shown so far is that linguistic universalism might seem at odds with relativity at first glance but offers interesting avenues for compatibility. While cognitive linguistics and 4E approaches to cognition might seem to more obviously provide a grounding for relativity, they go beyond linguistic relativity and might complicate the causal lines between language and cognition even further.

5.4 Large Language Models and Human Cognition

In this final exploration of the interface between cognitive science and linguistic relativity, we delve into a prominent contemporary issue in artificial intelligence, specifically with relation to natural language processing (NLP) and large language models (LLMs). The issue is

---

[16] Nothing we have said here is meant to favour one particular brand of linguistics or cognitive science over the other. We are merely exploring different theoretical foundations for a contemporary account of linguistic relativity.

whether or not LLMs 'understand' natural language. In effect, we will show that the current debate can be recast as a debate about linguistic relativity, with some interesting consequences.

Of course, Searle (1980) introduced the topic of understanding to the philosophical discussions of AI with his (in)famous Chinese room argument. In the original thought experiment, Searle finds himself inside a room with an instruction manual for converting strings of an unknown (to him) language into other strings. The rule-book is envisaged as some sort of symbolic calculus. In the same way that a computer processes binary code, the Searle inside the room takes shapes in and, via an algorithm in the GOFAI (good old-fashioned AI) tradition, outputs other shapes. Unbeknownst to Searle, however, the characters or shapes are Mandarin sentences and the rulebook are the syntactic rules of that language. Outside the room, Chinese patrons dutifully post their questions on various topics and receive intelligible answers. It's a bit like a lo-fi version of ChatGPT.

Searle—the philosopher, not his avatar—inside the thought experiment, asked us to ponder whether or not his avatar actually understands Chinese. The intuitive answer was clearly no. After dismissing a number of challenges, he concluded that 'Strong AI' imbued with human-level intelligence, understanding, and intentionality (perhaps consciousness too) was not possible, at least not with the technology available at the time of his writing (1980).

Things may have changed with the advent of deep learning technologies and especially the perhaps 'unreasonable effectiveness' of transformers in NLP (Vaswani et al., 2017). Modern AI has apparently surmounted the holy grail of syntactic competence in a way that was previously unimaginable. Artificial neural networks, powered by Big Data and advanced connectionist architecture, have produced seamless text, sentiment analysis, summarisation, code generation, translation, and a number of other linguistic applications. Any school teacher or college professor is well aware at this point of the pervasive use of these platforms in plagiarising text. In fact, given that these models are basically trained on the whole internet and the training sets are often undisclosed, it is not clear to what extent they themselves plagiarise in general. We will put issues of data contamination and memorisation to the side for present purposes.

The interesting point is that Searle's basic philosophical agenda has been revisited in the present AI context, especially in a much-discussed article by Bender and Koller (2020). In the article, they argue that LLMs are incapable of true understanding of human language because (modifying Searle) they are 'all syntax and no semantics'. In order to make their case, they move from one Chinese room to two desert islands, each with one marooned occupant. Each individual discovers an old abandoned telegraph machine and quickly establishes a literal line of communication with the other. The two interlocutors continue their correspondence for many years without ever discovering that a highly intelligent underwater octopus has been listening in on every exchange. This octopus, like an LLM, is equipped with a special ability to pick up on statistical patterns in the signal. In fact it is so good that at some point it completely cuts one of the islanders off and substitutes itself surreptitiously into the exchange with the other.

Eventually, according to Bender and Koller (2020), the octopus's mimicry of human communication (or 'weak AI' in Searle's terminology) will give out. As a matter of fact, this point comes when one islander is faced with an imminent threat and asks what she thinks is the other islander for assistance with fashioning some sort of weapon for protection. Since all the octopus has been trained on is (telegraphed) speech and it has never encountered any objects in the domain of either speaker, it cannot, Bender and Koller argue, understand such reference or intentionality. That thing that makes humans' thoughts and words be *about* objects and situations in the environment is what is missing along with a few other things. This, along with communicative intent, is essential for linguistic meaning.

Since then, a cottage industry of philosophers collaborating with NLP researchers have taken this argument as a challenge (Cappelen and Dever, 2021, Mandelkern and Linzen, 2024, Ohmer et al., 2024). The central question has been whether or not such reference is accessible to LLMs trained only on massive amounts of compressed text. Frege was resurrected, Kripke got a callout, and Wittgenstein is never too far from any conversation about language. We won't directly get into the 'understanding' debate here. Rather we suggest that one possible interpretation of the debate touches the linguistic relativity issue directly and in doing so can shed light on the overarching question about the human-language-using capabilities of modern LLMs.

Basically, it's a lesson in comparative cognition. For the first time in human history, some other system (besides humans) is able to generate and potentially even grasp the complexity of natural language. For years, linguists, primatologists, and evolutionary biologists have postulated language-like mechanisms in other species, from songbirds to chimpanzees and most recently to sperm whales (Begus et al., 2023). But actual human speech and writing have eluded even the most complex creatures on the planet. Where organic life seems to have fallen short of that gold standard, AI has recently risen to the challenge with some aplomb. Transformer-based platforms such as GPT-4, GPT-4o, and Gemini are able to not only answer prompts but also generate essay-length sentences covering a range of topics in a number of distinct voices. You could ask ChatGPT to explain entropy in a Shakespearean sonnet and it will produce intricate physics in iambic pentameter.[17]

Returning to the issue at hand, Bender and Koller's reason for denying that the octopus can understand or access meaning centres around whether or not something trained only on form or text can be said to acquire a language rich with word-to-world relations (Bender and Koller, 2020). The world of the octopus contains no chairs, tables, knives, or bears. Most LLMs 'see' only large amounts of flattened text and process vector (rows and columns of numbers) representations of language by means of weighted connections between millions of nodes and an ingenious loss function that backtracks while correcting connections along to way to the delivery of the desired target values. So the question becomes: can a creature or system truly understand human language without a human's worldview?

Let us go back to the argument we made in §5.2.1 that different UGs would generate different worldviews by constraining the cognitive capacities of the creatures in their possession. We mentioned

---

[17] This isn't to oversell the technology. There are still some serious issues of epistemic opacity and hallucinations, in which syntactically well-formed but inexplicably mendacious text is generated.

Martians and heptopods. They might indeed see the world differently or see our languages differently from the way we do. In essence, Bender and Koller (2020)'s challenge is that even if LLMs can mimic human language, they don't have the right kind of cognition to understand it. Furthermore, if our language is shaped by the environment into which we are thrust at birth and this environment in turn conditions our cognitive capabilities via that language (as per *Grand Relativism*), then no creature without those experiences can extract the meaning from the mere sounds, strings of sound, or even distributional relationships among those strings (as the LLMs might be seen as doing). We have seen a similar view emerge from the embodied and enactive literature in cognitive linguistics. There's a feedback loop between language, cognition, and the environment such that removing one component renders the others inaccessible. This much universalists and cognitive linguists can agree on.[18]

Thus, linguistic relativity can provide an answer to a puzzle concerning meaning in machines. Even without the Grand Relativism claim, language can structure thought in myriad ways. Language understanding is, then, partly based on complex interactions in an environment both physical and linguistic, that is, communication with other people. The kinds of LLMs under discussion lack all of these features. In other words, to them we might be like the persistent caricature of the Inuits, with their supposedly countless words for snow, in that we have no access to the icy substance at the genesis. Such a caricature can analyse and even predict the next snowy word but cannot access the worldview that goes along with it because it has never itself encountered a flake.

Of course, these ruminations need some qualification. The fact that current LLMs process large amounts of text exclusively isn't an essential property. More and more research is exploring multimodal datasets which include video, audio, and pictorial files. Some promising research avenues, such as BabyLM, has even limited the size of datasets so as to be model actual human language acquisition and the

---

[18] The precise degrees of influence is another matter.

poverty of stimulus. Slowly, we aim to introduce the octopus into our world.[19]

At this point it might be useful to consider a recent article by Google researcher Blaise Agüera y Arcas, who argues that LLMs like LaMDA and GPT-3 can access concepts like colour through association with language. This is the case, he claims, because concepts themselves are mere 'correlations, associations, and generalization' (Agüera y Arcas, 2022, p. 188). Here he draws on the reported experience of the remarkable Helen Keller, who, through language, really saw the world in a different way. We'll leave you with her words:

> for me, too, there is exquisite color. I have a color scheme that is my own. I will try to explain what I mean: Pink makes me think of a baby's cheek, or a gentle southern breeze. Lilac, which is my teacher's favorite color, makes me think of faces I have loved and kissed. There are two kinds of red for me. One is the red of warm blood in a healthy body; the other is the red of hell and hate. I like the first red because of its vitality. In the same way, there are two kinds of brown. One is alive – the rich, friendly brown of earth mold; the other is a deep brown, like the trunks of old trees with wormholes in them, or like withered hands. Orange gives me a happy, cheerful feeling, partly because it is bright and partly because it is friendly to so many other colors. Yellow signifies abundance to me. I think of the yellow sun streaming down, it means life and is rich in promise. Green means exuberance. The warm sun brings out odors that make me think of red; coolness brings out odors that make me think of green.

---

[19] In the other direction, the Explainable AI movement can be seen as an attempt by us to comprehend the alternative worldview of the aliens already among us.

6

Conclusion: Whorf and Relativity—Yes? or No?

6.1 No!

There seem to be two broad strategies that lie behind No! to linguistic relativity:

- The claim (à la Kant?) that we all have precisely the same *mental structures* that are governed the same way, resulting in just the very same concepts for anyone, no matter what sort of environmental differences there may be. One's language just maps onto that, no matter how different language X might be from language Y.
- The claim (à la Chomsky?) that we all have identical *language faculties*, and that given the "fact" that the world/environment is (essentially) the same for us all, this identical-for-everyone language faculty will generate (essentially) the same mental structures/concepts.

The "sameness" mentioned in these two general strategies might each be only "approximations" and so there can be *some* differences, and *some* of the items under consideration can be codified differently in different languages. But these will be "small" differences, easily recognized as such, and easily altered in any person's mind.

Behind these thoughts lie the convictions that either (or both) (a) (almost?) all mental structures in humans are fundamentally the same across cultures and environments, or (b) all languages are (almost?) identical, due to all humans having the same language-acquisition module. And while there can be some "small" differences, from the fact that people can learn very different foreign languages it follows that any such differences are of no real consequence and do not imply linguistic relativity.

6.2 Yes!

Linguistic relativity seems to be a consequence of denying both of the No! strategies. In other words, linguistic relativists

- believe that there are (classes of) languages that are very radically different from one another.
- believe that, as different children learn different languages, this can give rise to very different mental internalizations of "ambiguous" external sense experiences, dependent on how different the languages are. Hence, the presumed radically different languages will generate different ways to "understand" or "categorize" or "label" the external world.

The "ambiguous external sense experiences" are a nod to the claims of Sapir and Whorf, mentioned in §3.2 and §3.4, concerning the "kaleidoscopic flux of impressions" (Whorf) and "incommensurable analyses of experience in different languages" (Sapir).

Now, it seems completely clear that there are languages that are totally different from one another, and radically so. As Sapir illustrated, and has been confirmed by many other Americanist linguists, many of these languages treat (almost all) SAE nominal constructions as verbal constructions. As mentioned in §3.6.2, this is a main point of dispute between Whorf's and Malotki's remarks about Hopi time. Malotki translates *payi-s-tota* as *they did it three times* whereas Whorf translates such sentences as *they did three repetitions*. Given that the sentence is not making a nominalization that "designates a thing", the sentence should be seen as a verbal construction: it would seem that Whorf has the more accurate, and more true to Hopi, translation.

7
Afterword

7.1 Linguistic Relativity through the Ages

Linguistic relativity did not start with Benjamin Whorf, but had a much earlier pedigree... despite the fact that Whorf might not have been aware of it.

Our first three chapters told a tale of a certain "feeling" on the part of a number of thinkers ... starting with a mention of remarks by some ancient Greek philosophers ... arose—that there was some "deep connection" between the language one spoke and the type of thoughts one could have. And as a consequence of this connection, there was (or could be) a discrepancy between one's thoughts and the way "reality" was. However, detailed discussion about this underlying idea did not enter the intellectual world until an opposing conception was more carefully adumbrated by Immanuel Kant.

Sapir, Whorf's mentor, was certainly aware of at least some of this history, as is evidenced by his M.A. thesis on Johann von Herder. As we said in Chapter 3, Herder's later work a view divergent from Kant's apparent view that all people have the same psychological abilities and will end up with the same results in their use of reason. At the very least, a view such as Herder's would allow people to come to different conceptual conclusions from different types of experiences. And that is at least one apparently necessary aspect of the linguistic relativity position. However, we think that the attack on Kantian mental faculties does not fully capture the import of linguistic relativity: for that, one needs clear evidence of the different observable results brought about by being speakers of radically different languages. And Herder—while he was fluent in most European languages—just didn't have the knowledge of the "exotic" languages that Whorf drew his inspiration from.

Knowledge of the vastly different grammatical structures in some languages became more widely known with the European explorations into the Americas (as well as the Pacific), and we have drawn attention to the collection of (partial) grammars of languages of the Americas that Alexander von Humboldt sent to his brother Wilhelm von Humboldt. Wilhelm's analysis of these grammars led to the recognition of just how different many of the world's languages are from those of Europe, and his speculations on how this might in turn cause different world views drew considerable interest. But here, also, we find that the lack of direct insight and information regarding the specific types of cultures that were associated with the specific different languages prevented him from adequately giving any sort of theory from which one could predict the influence of language on worldview—as would be required from an account of linguistic relativity.

From there we moved to figures who did have more direct experience of the "exotic languages" and the cultures of the speakers: Franz Boas and Edward Sapir. We deemed Boas not to have fully made the inference to linguistic relativity of these speakers, but we noted that Sapir had made such a move in midcareer. That development became even more notable in Whorf, who advanced various theories about what aspects of languages (including "hidden" aspects) might give rise to such-and-so specific differences in 'world view' between speakers of these 'exotic languages' and speakers of European languages. And it was these sorts of explanations and inferences that became known as Whorfianism—perhaps a particular form of linguistic relativity. Certainly Whorf's publication of his findings in MIT's *Technology Review* made his viewpoint rather more widely known than had he published them in technical linguistic-anthropology journals.

Harry Hoijer, another student of Sapir, carried on Whorf's project after Whorf's death, bringing it to the attention of prominent linguists and anthropologists. In turn, this attention was further broadened by these scholars within their own professions, and it ultimately brought forth a number of attempts to 'scientifically examine' whether "the Whorf hypothesis" was true.

That story continues with many further attempts to prove or discredit linguistic relativity, as we've discussed in the subsequent chapters. We think that one very important issue that has not received the attention it deserves is that of translation from one to another language. As we remarked in §3.6.2, there is always an issue concerning the best way to translate from Language A to Language B when there are grammatical differences between the two. Simple examples we've cited concern mass versus count assignments: do we follow the way Language A employs this distinction, or is it a better translation to change it to the way it would be done in Language B? In the case of more notable grammatical distinctions between languages—for example, the grammatical fact that various Amerindian languages do not distinguish a class of nouns from a class of verbs but European languages do, should we try to honour the grammar and its presuppositions of Language A? Or should we "make a guess" of how a speaker of Language B might describe "the same scene"? Note that choosing one way or the other already amounts to denying or validating the position that different languages "carve up reality differently". Related to this issue is the emic-versus-etic distinction: do we translate in a such a way as to describe the relevant situation "from the point of view of a member of the community" or "from the point of view of an outside observer of the situation"?

7.2 Whorfianism and Linguistic Relativity

The journey from Whorfianism to linguistic relativity has taken many twists and turns. In Chapter 4, we presented a continuum from minor to grand relativism via a medial type. The cluster of claims that form this medial layer of analysis seems to dovetail with much of the literature on the topic. In their review article, Reines and Prinz (2009) advocate what they call "habitual Whorfianism" or the view that languages only influence our psychological processes through instilling habitual mechanisms of thought as special kinds of language-specific 'defaults'. Although they entertain a stronger ontological version as well, they claim that much of the current literature and experimentation can safely be explained by reference to the "habitual" variety of linguistic relativity

Seuren (2013) takes a similar approach to the retrieving of any insight from Whorf's ideas. In fact, he distinguishes between Whorfianism and linguistic relativity in a manner we have implicitly practised here but not explicitly mentioned. He associates linguistic relativity with strong claims of diversity (such as those made by Evans and Levinson, 2009). This view, for him, is incompatible with universalism in a way that Whorfianism is not. Essentially, his view agrees with ours on the possibility of universalism and different UGs (although he doesn't consider that possibility). His positive account splits cognition into a core and a periphery. The peripheral system is largely automatic and unconscious. Here, frequency of patterns can obviate the need for engagement with core or 'central' thought processes. This is a matter of cognitive efficiency. The best chance Whorfianism has, for Seuren, lies in the peripheral systems of cognition. Routine formation, aimed at reducing attentional effort, is the most likely target of the influence of specific language forms. The conscious deliberative mental activities, and the 'universal, species-specific, residue of central cognition' (p. 30), are relatively immune to the vagaries of linguistic structure. He calls his theory 'provisional and hypothetical' but marks it as a useful framework. Of course, according to prominent psychologists, for example Kahneman (2011), cognition is indeed bifurcated between a 'system 1' which is rapid and intuitive (what Seuren calls 'peripheral') and 'system 2' which is more conscious, logical, and deliberative (Seuren's 'core'). Again, the possibilities which surround relativism are of the medial variety. Routine patterns, habits, defaults form the most plausible routes for language to influence cognition. We concur.

The problem stronger versions of relativity face is what McWhorter (2014) dubs 'bubbling'. Languages, the world over, bubble and fizz in ways not isomorphic to their environments. A language spoken in Australasian can contain evidentials in the same way that one spoken in Sub-Saharan Africa can without any similar environmental or cultural conditions. The reverse holds as well. Some similar cultures carve up the world with noncongruous linguistic patterns. Structure emerges for a variety of reasons and, as McWhorter carefully points out, these reasons very often have little to do with the descriptive needs of the given community or the unique circumstances in which they find themselves. This is part of the reason that grander versions of linguistic relativity seem to survive only in science fiction settings. They are indeed conceivable or even logically possible but mainly for beings quite unlike ourselves in worlds markedly dissimilar from our own.

In Chapter 5 we explored how twentieth- and twenty-first-century cognitive science (broadly construed) has engaged with linguistic relativity. Once more, the medial version seems to be the most prominent and effervescent instantiation of the idea. The thesis that language influences or determines cognition is a claim that emerged from philosophy and early linguistic anthropology and eventually found renewal within experimental cognitive anthropology.

We showed that despite some family resemblance between claims of the linguistic turn and linguistic relativity, the two movements ultimately diverge on empirical grounds. Philosophers were focused on how language can unearth universal truths. Their general arsenal was limited to a few SAE languages with a predominantly English bias—while relativists embraced genuine linguistic diversity and rejected universalism. This latter rejection is taken for granted in much of the literature, but we show that two possibilities might hold for the compatibility of linguistic relativity and a specific account of universalism given in Chomskyan linguistics. However, if a ranking between these constraints were forced, universalism would take priority over relativity in the theory. The room for relativity is thus circumscribed within generative grammar.

If we move from the strictures of generative linguistics to typology and cognitive linguistics the picture begins to change. Typology involves the mandatory recognition of radical linguistic diversity while cognitive linguistics encompasses a more general (non-domain-specific) approach to cognition. Combined, they seem to provide a fertile ground for linguistic relativity and its kin, at least prima facie. Our analysis surveyed stronger and stronger claims as to the constitutive connection between cognition and the world from Embedded to Enactive varieties. The interesting product of this peregrination was the recognition that more radical noncomputationalist perspectives on cognition do entail linguistic relativity even if they potentially endorse other forms of relativity in addition. One reason for this consequence is that language—unlike the classical cognitive revolution in which language was central—plays a more peripheral role in these theories.

Lastly, we applied our newly honed distinctions to the question of understanding in contemporary AI, specifically with relation to LLMs. We transposed this debate into one that asks whether human language understanding is indeed possible without a human environment to reference (or to learn to reference). This is essentially a question about linguistic relativity. The existence of complex machines that seem to be able to grasp our intricate meanings has propelled relativity into current and future debates in AI, although every aspect of such claims is highly contested in the contemporary discourse.

Whatever your position is on the issue of effects that language(s) have on thought, there is simply no denying that these questions are, and will be, pervasive in contemporary cognitive science and future theories of the relationships between mind, language, and reality.

Bibliography

Aarsleff, H. (1982a). *From Locke to Saussure: Essays on the Study of Language and Intellectual History*. Minneapolis: University of Minnesota Press.

Aarsleff, H. (1982b). Introduction. In (Aarsleff, 1982a, pp. vii–lxv).

Aarsleff, H. (1988). Introduction. In (von Humboldt, 1836, pp. vii–lxv).

Agüera y Arcas, B. (2022). Do large language models understand us? *Daedalus 151*, 183–197.

Allan, K. (2010). *The Western Classical Tradition in Linguistics*. London: Equinox. 2nd ed. of 2007 book; much expanded.

Au, T. K.-F. (1984a). Chinese and English counterfactuals: The Sapir-Whorf hypothesis revisited. *Cognition 15*, 275–287.

Au, T. K.-F. (1984b). Counterfactuals: In reply to Alfred Bloom. *Cognition 17*, 289–302.

Bach, E. (1986a). The algebra of events. *Linguistics and Philosophy 9*, 5–16.

Bach, E. (1986b). Natural language metaphysics. In R. Marcus, G. Dorn, and P. Weingartner (Eds.), *Logic, Methodology, and Philosophy of Science, VII*, pp. 573–595. Amsterdam: North-Holland.

Bach, E. (1994). The semantics of syntactic categories: A cross-linguistic perspective. In J. Macnamara and G. Reyes (Eds.), *The Logical Foundations of Cognition*, pp. 264–281. New York: Oxford University Press.

Bach, E. (1995). A note on quantification and blankets in Haisla. In E. Bach, E. Jelinek, A. Kratzer, and B. Partee (Eds.), *Quantification in Natural Languages*, pp. 13–20. Dordrecht: Kluwer.

Bach, E. (1996). The politics of universal grammar.Linguistic Society of America Presidential Address.

Bach, E. (2007). Deixis in Northern Wakashan. In P. Austin and A. Simpson (Eds.), *Endangered Languages*, pp. 253–265. Weisbaden: VS Verlag für Sozialwissenschften. *Linguistische Berichte* Sonderhefte 14.

Bach, E.E, and W. Chao (2012). The metaphysics of natural language(s). In R. Kempson, T. Fernando, and N. Asher (Eds.), *Handbook of the Philosophy of Science. Volume 14: Philosophy of Linguistics*, pp. 175–196. Amsterdam: Elsevier.

Baghramian, M. and J. A. Carter (2022). Relativism. In E. N. Zalta (Ed.), *The Stanford Encyclopedia of Philosophy* (Winter 2023 ed.). Metaphysics Research Lab, Stanford University. See https://plato.stanford.edu/archives/win2023/entries/relativism/. Their discussion of Whorfianism is in their xxx00A7;4.1, "Cultural relativism".

Baker, M. (1995). *The Polysynthesis Parameter*. Oxford, UK: Oxford University Press.

Barnes, M. (1975). *Linguistics and Language in Science-Fiction Fantasy*. New York: Arno Press.

Barrett, L. (2018). The evolution of cognition: A 4E perspective. In A. Newen, L. De Bruin, and S. Gallagher (Eds.), *The Oxford Handbook of 4E Cognition*, pp. 623-640. Oxford, UK: Oxford University Press.

Barthes, R. (1983). *The Empire of Signs*. New York: Hill & Wang. English translation of Barthes's 1970 *L'Empire des signes*.

Beaney, M. (Ed.) (2013). *The Oxford Handbook of the History of Analytic Philosophy*. Oxford, UK: Oxford University Press.

Begus, G., R. Sprouse, A. Leban, M. Silva, and S. Gero (2023, Dec). Vowels and diphthongs in sperm whales. OSF Preprints; osf.io/285cs; DOI: 10.31219/osf.io/285cs.

Bender, E. and A. Koller (2020). Climbing towards NLU: On meaning, form, and understanding in the age of data. In *Proceedings of the 59th Annual Meeting of the Association for Computational Linguistics*, Online, pp. 5185-5198. Association for Computational Linguistics.

Bergman, G. (1952). Two types of linguistic philosophy. *Review of Metaphysics 5*(3), 417-438.

Berwick, R. and N. Chomsky (2016). *Why Only Us?* New York: MIT Press.

Black, M. (1956). Review of *Language in Culture* by Harry Hoijer. *Philosophical Review 65*, 413-418.

Black, M. (1969). Some troubles with Whorfianism. In S. Hook (Ed.), *Language and Philosophy: A Symposium*, pp. 30-35. New York: New York University Press.

Bloom, A. (1981). *The Linguistic Shaping of Thought: A Study in the Impact of Language on Thinking in China and the West*. Hillsdale, NJ: Lawrence Erlbaum.

Bloom, A. (1984). Caution - The words you use may affect what you say: A response to Terry Kit-fong Au's "Chinese and English counterfactuals: The Sapir-Whorf hypothesis revisited". *Cognition 17*, 275-287.

Bloomfield, L. (1933). *Language*. New York: Holt.

Boas, F. (1911). *The Mind of Primitive Man*. New York: Macmillan.

Boas, F. (1912a). Changes in the bodily form of descendants of immigrants. *American Anthropologist 14*, 530-562.

Boas, F. (1912b). The history of the American race. *Annals of the New York Academy of Sciences 21*, 177-183.

Boas, F., and L. Müller-Wille (1998). *Franz Boas among the Inuit of Baffin Island, 1883-1884: Journals and Letters*. Toronto: University of Toronto Press. Edited & introduced by Ludger Müller-Wille; translated by William Barr.

Boeckx, C. (2005). Generative grammar and modern cognitive science. *Journal of Cognitive Science 6*, 45-54.

Bohnemeyer, J. (2002). Review of Pütz and Verspoor (2000). *Language and Society 31*, 452-456.

Boroditsky, L. (2001). Does language shape thought? Mandarin and English speakers' conceptions of time. *Cognitive Psychology 43*, 1-22.

Boroditsky, L., O. Fuhrman, and K. McKormick (2011). Do English and Mandarin speakers think about time differently? *Cognition 118*, 123-129.

Boroditsky, L. (2003). Linguistic relativity. In L. Nadel (Ed.), *Encyclopedia of Cognitive Science*, pp. 917-921. MacMillan.

Boroditsky, L., L. Schmidt, and W. Phillips (2003). Sex, syntax, and semantics. In D. Gentner and S. Goldin-Meadow (Eds.), *Language in Mind: Advances in the Study of Language and Thought*, pp. 61-79. Cambridge, MA: MIT Press.

Bowerman, M., and S. Levinson (2001). *Language Acquisition and Conceptual Development*. Cambridge, UK: Cambridge University Press.

Brown, R. (1967). *Wilhelm von Humboldt's Conception of Linguistic Relativity*. The Hague: Mouton.

Bylund, E. and P. Athanasopoulos (2017). The Whorfian time warp: Representing duration through the language hourglass. *Journal of Experimental Psychology: General 146*, 911–916.

Cappelen, H., and J. Dever (2021). *Making AI Intelligible*. Oxford, UK: Oxford University Press.

Carnap, R. (1950). Empiricism, semantics and ontology. *Revue Internationale de Philosophie* 4(11), 20–40.

Carroll, J. (1956a). Introduction. In (Carroll, 1956b, 1–34).

Carroll, J. (Ed.) (1956b). *Language, Thought, and Reality: Selected Writings of Benjamin Lee Whorf*. Cambridge, MA: MIT Press. A Second Edition of this volume, slightly altered, is Carroll et al. (2012).

Carroll, J. (2012). Introduction. In (Carroll et al., 2012, pp. 1–43).

Carroll, J., S. Levinson, and P. Lee (Eds.) (2012). *Language, Thought and Reality: Selected Writings of Benjamin Lee Whorf; Second Edition*. Cambridge, MA: MIT Press. This "updated version" of Carroll (1956b) has a new "Forward" (Levinson, 2012), an expanded editorial group, and a newly-added work of Whorf's as an Appendix, "The Yale Report"

Casasanto, D., L. Boroditsky, W. Phillips, J. Greene, S. Goswami, S. Bocanegra-Thiel, and D. Gil (2004). How deep are effects of language on thought? Time estimation in speakers of English, Indonesian, Greek and Spanish. In K. Forbus, D. Gentner, and T. Reigier (Eds.), *Proceedings of the 26th Annual Conference of the Cognitive Science Society*, Mahwah, NJ, pp. 186–191. Lawrence Erlbaum.

Cassirer, E. (1933). La Langue et la construction du monde des objets. *Journal de psychologie normale et de pathologie 30*, 18–44.

Cavell, S. (1976). *Must We Mean What We Say?: A Book of Essays*. New York: Cambridge University Press.

Cheng, W. (1985). Pictures of ghosts: A critique of Alfred Bloom's *The Linguistic Shaping of Thought*. *American Anthropologist 87*, 917–922.

Chomsky, N. (1975). *Reflections on Language*. New York: Pantheon Books.

Chomsky, N. (1980). *Rules and Representations*. New York: Columbia University Press.

Chomsky, N. (2000). *New Horizons in the Study of Language and Mind*. New York: Cambridge University Press.

Cimpian, A. and S.-J. Leslie (2017). The brilliance trap. *Scientific American 317*(3), 60–65.

Clark, A. and D. J. Chalmers (1998). The extended mind. *Analysis 58*(1), 7–19.

Clark, R. (1955). *Herder: His Life and Thought*. Berkeley and Los Angeles: University of California Press.

Clifford, W. K. (1880). *Seeing and Thinking*. London: MacMillan & Co. Accessed via Google Books: https://play.google.com/store/books/details?id=Ux7uKx_I1IcC&rdid=book-Ux7uKx_I1IcC&rdot=1.

Cole, D. (1999). *Franz Boas: The Early Years, 1859–1906*. Seattle: University of Washington Press.

Cole, D. and L. Müller-Wille (1984). Franz Boas' expedition to Baffin Island 1883–1884. *Études/Inuit/Studies 8*, 37–63.
Croft, W. (2013). Radical Construction Grammar. In *The Oxford Handbook of Construction Grammar*. Oxford, UK: Oxford University Press.
Darnell, R. (1990). *Edward Sapir: Linguist, Anthropologist, Humanist*. Lincoln: University of Nebraska Press. Second edition, with new introduction, 2010.
Darnell, R. (1998). Camelot at Yale: The construction and dismantling of the Sapirian synthesis, 1931-39. *American Anthropologist 100*, 361–372.
Davidson, D. (1973). On the very idea of a conceptual scheme. *Proceedings and Addresses of the American Philosophical Association 47*, 5–20.
Davidson, D. (1986). A nice derangement of epitaphs. In E. LePore (Ed.), *Truth and Interpretation: Perspectives on the Philosophy of Donald Davidson*, pp. 433–446. Blackwell.
Deutscher, G. (2010). *The Language Glass: Why the World Looks Different in Other Languages*. New York: Henry Holt.
Dinwoodie, D. (2006). Time and the individual in Native North America. In P. Strong, and S. Kan (Eds.), *New Perspectives on Native North America: Cultures, Histories, and Representations*, pp. 327–348. Lincoln: : University of Nebraska Press.
Dove, G. O. (2022). Rethinking the role of language in embodied cognition. *Philosophical Transactions of the Royal Society B: Biological Sciences 378*(1870), 20210375. DOI: 10.1098/rstb.2021.0375
Dummett, M. (1978). *Truth and Other Enigmas*. Cambridge, MA: : Harvard University Press.
Edwards, R. (2017). The Sapir-Whorf hypothesis: Reflections of modernity in the borderlands of the United States. Available through https://www.researchgate.net/publication/323457767_The_Sapir-Whorf_Hypothesis_Reflections_of_Modernity_in_the_Borderlands_of_the_United_States.
Elgin, S. H. (1972). The crossover constraint and Ozark English. In J. Kimball (Ed.), *Syntax and Semantics, Vol. 1*, pp. 267–275. Amsterdam: Brill.
Elgin, S. H. (1979). *What is Linguistics?* Englewood Cliffs, N.J: Prentice-Hall.
Ellis, J. (1993). *Language, Thought, and Logic*. Evanston, IL:Northwestern University Press.
Enfield, N. (2000). On linguocentrism. In (Pütz and Verspoor, 2000, pp. 125–157).
Evans, N. and S. C. Levinson (2009). The myth of language universals: Language diversity and its importance for cognitive science. *Behavioral and Brain Sciences 32*(5), 429–448.
Everett, D. (2005). Cultural constraints on grammar and cognition in Pirahã. *Current Anthropology 46*, 621–646.
Feng, G. and L. Yi (2006). What if Chinese had linguistic markers for counterfactual conditionals? Language and thought revisited. *Proceedings of the 28th Annual Conference of the Cognitive Science Society 28*, 1281–1286.
Fodor, J. (1975). *The Language of Thought*. New York: Crowell.
Forster, M. (2010a). *After Herder: Philosophy of Language in the German Tradition*. Oxford, UK: Oxford University Press. See especially Chapter 6.
Forster, M. (2010b). *German Philosophy of Language: From Schlegel to Hegel and Beyond*. Oxford, UK: Oxford University Press. See especially Chapter 4.

Forster, M. (2012). Kant's philosophy of language? *Tijdschrift voor Filosofie 74*, 485–511.

Forster, M. (2022). Johann Gottfried von Herder. In E. N. Zalta (Ed.), *The Stanford Encyclopedia of Philosophy*. Metaphysics Research Lab, Stanford University. https://plato.stanford.edu/archives/sum2022/entries/herder/.

Foster-Hanson, E., S. J. Leslie, and M. Rhodes (2016). How does generic language elicit essentialist beliefs? In A. Papafragou, D. Grodner, D. Mirman, and J. C. Trueswell (Eds.), *Proceedings of the 38th Annual Conference of the Cognitive Science Society.*, pp. 1541–1546. Austin, TX: Cognitive Science Society.

Gentner, D. and S. Goldin-Meadow (2003). Whither Whorf. In D. Gentner and S. Goldin-Meadow (Eds.), *Language in Mind: Advances in the Study of Language and Cognition*, pp. 3–14. Cambridge, MA: MIT Press.

Gladstone, W. (1858). *Studies on Homer and the Homeric Age*. Vol. *I*. Oxford, UK: Oxford University Press.

Gladstone, W. (1877). The colour sense. *Nineteenth Century 2*, 366–388.

Goldberg, A. (2015). Compositionality. In *Routledge Semantics Handbook*. Routledge.

Greenberg, J. (1954). Concerning inferences from linguistic to nonlinguistic data. In (Hoijer, 1954a, pp.3–19).

Griffith-Dickson, G. (2022). Johann Georg Hamann. In E. N. Zalta (Ed.), *The Stanford Encyclopedia of Philosophy*. https://plato.stanford.edu/archives/spr2022/entries/hamann/.

Gronemeyer, C. (1996). Noun incorporation in Hopi. *Lund University, Dept. Linguistics Working Papers 45*, 25–44.

Hacker, P. (2007). Analytic philosophy: Beyond the linguistic turn and back again. In M. Beaney (Ed.), *The Analytic Turn*, pp. 125–141. New York: Routledge.

Hacker, P. (2013). The linguistic turn in analytic philosophy. In M. Beaney (Ed.), *The Oxford Handbook of The History of Analytic Philosophy*, pp. 926–947. Oxford, UK: Oxford University Press.

Haslanger, S. (2012). *Resisting Reality: Social Construction and Social Critique*. Oxford, UK: Oxford University Press.

Haspelmath, M. (2019). Ergativity and depth of analysis. *Rhema*, 108–130.

Haßler, G. (2006). 18th century linguistic thought. In K. Brown (Ed.), *Encyclopedia of Language & Linguistics*, 2nd Edition, pp. 88–94. Oxford: Elsevier.

Haun, D., C. Rapold, G. Janzen, and S. Levinson (2011). Plasticity of human spatial cognition: Spatial language and cognition covary across cultures. *Cognition 119*, 70–80.

Hauser, M., N. Chomsky, and W. T. Fitch (2002). The faculty of language: What is it, who has it, and how did it evolve? *Science 298*(22), 1569–1579.

Haviland, J. (1998). Guugu Yimithirr cardinal directions. *Ethos 26*, 7–24.

Heijenoort, J. (1967). Logic as calculus and logic as language. *Synthese 17*(1), 324–330.

Hill, D. (1997). Finding your way in Longgu: Geographical reverence in a Solomon Island language. In G. Senft (Ed.), *Referring to Space: Studies in Austronesian and Papual Languages*, pp. 101–126. Oxford: Clarendon Press.

Hill, J. (1988). Language, culture, and world view. In F. Newmeyer (Ed.), *Linguistics: The Cambridge Survey. Vol. 4: Language: The Socio-Cultural Context*, pp. 14–36. Cambridge, UK: Cambridge University Press.

Hill, J. and B. Mannheim (1992). Language and world view. *Annual Review of Anthropology 21*, 381–406.

Hinton, L. (1988). Review of Malotki (1983). *American Indian Quarterly 12*, 361–364.

Hoijer, H. (1946). *Linguistic Structures of Native America*. New York: Wenner-Gren Foundation for Anthropological Research.

Hoijer, H. (1951). Cultural implications of some Navaho linguistic categories. *Language 27*, 111–120.

Hoijer, H. (1953). The relation of language to culture. In A. Kroeber (Ed.), *Anthropology Today: An Encyclopedic Inventory*, pp. 554–584. Chicago: University of Chicago Press.

Hoijer, H. (Ed.) (1954a). *Language in Culture: Proceedings of a Conference on the Interrelations of Language and Other Aspects of Culture*. Chicago: University of Chicago Press. Also published by the American Anthropological Association as *American Anthropologist*, volume 56, no. 6, part 2, December 1954. Besides seven papers presented at the conference, there is a very lengthy transcription of nine sessions of discussions.

Hoijer, H. (1954b). The Sapir-Whorf hypothesis. In (Hoijer, 1954a, pp. 92–105).

Hsu, C. (2013). Counterfactual reasoning embodied in cognition rather than linguistic forms: Evidence from a developmental study in Chinese. *Journal of Chinese Linguistics 41*, 292–316.

Hukari, T. (1976). Person in a Coast Salish language. *International Journal of American Linguistics 42*, 305–318.

Isaac, M. G., S. Koch, and R. Nefdt (2022). Conceptual engineering: A road map to practice. *Philosophy Compass 17*, 1–15.

Jaing, Y. (2019). Chinese counterfactual reasoning. In C.-R. Huang, Z. Jing-Schmidt, and B. Meisterernst (Eds.), *The Routledge Handbook of Chinese Applied Linguistics*, pp. 276–293. London: Routledge.

January, D. and E. Kako (2007). Re-evaluating evidence for linguistic relativity: Reply to Boroditsky (2001). *Cognition 104*, 417–26.

Jelinek, E. (1993). Prepositions in Straits Salish and the Noun/Verb question. In *Papers for the 28th International Conference on Salish and Neighboring Languages*. Seattle: University of Washington.

Jelinek, E. (1995). Quantification in Straits Salish. In E. Bach, E. Jelinek, A. Kratzer, and B. Partee (Eds.), *Quantification in Natural Languages*, pp. 487–540. Dordrecht: Kluwer.

Jelinek, E. and R. Demers (1994). Predicates and pronominal arguments in Straits Salish. *Language 70*, 697–736.

Johnson, M. (2018). The embodiment of language. In A. Newen, L. De Bruin, and S. Gallagher (Eds.), *The Oxford Handbook of 4E Cognition*, pp. 623–640. Oxford, UK: Oxford University Press.

Johnson, M. and G. Lakoff (2002). Why cognitive linguistics requires embodied realism. *Cognitive Linguistics 13*, 245–263.

Joos, M. (Ed.) (1966). *Readings in Linguistics I: The Development of Descriptive Linguistics in America 1925–56* (Fourth ed.). Chicago: University of Chicago Press.

Joseph, J. (1996). The immediate sources of the 'Sapir-Whorf hypothesis'. *Historiographia Linguistica 23*, 365–404.

Kahneman, D. (2011). *Thinking, Fast and Slow*. New York: New York: Farrar, Straus and Giroux.

Kinkade, D. (1983). Salish evidence on the universality of "Noun" and "Verb". *Lingua 60*, 25–40.

Knötsch, C. (1993). Franz Boas' research trip to Baffin Island 1882–1884. *Polar Geography and Geology 17*, 3–54.

Koerner, K. (1992). The Sapir-Whorf hypothesis: A preliminary history and a bibliographical essay. *Journal of Linguistic Anthropology 2*, 173–198. An updated and expanded version of this work appears as Chapter 10 of Koerner (1995), pp. 203–240.

Koerner, K. (1995). *Professing Linguistic Historiography*. Amsterdam: John Benjamins.

Koerner, K. (2000). Towards a full pedigree of the Sapir-Whorf hypothesis: From Locke to Lucy. In (Pütz and Verspoor, 2000, pp. 1–24).

Kousta, S., D. Vinson, and G. Vigliocco (2008). Investigating linguistic relativity through bilingualism: The case of grammatical gender. *Journal of Experimental Psychology: Learning, Memory, and Cognition 34*, 843–858.

Ladyman, J. and D. Ross (2007). *Every Thing Must Go: Metaphysics Naturalized*. New York: Oxford University Press.

Lakoff, G. and M. Johnson (1980). *Metaphors We Live By*. Chicago: Chicago University Press.

Leavitt, J. (2010). *Linguistic Relativities: Language Diversity and Modern Thought*. Cambridge, UK: Cambridge University Press.

Lee, P. (1991). Whorf's Hopi tensors: Subtle articulators in the language/thought nexus? *Cognitive Linguistics 2*, 123–147.

Lee, P. (1996). *The Whorf Theory Complex: A Critical Reconstruction*. Amsterdam: Benjamins.

Lee, P. (2000). When is linguistic relativity Whorf's linguistic relativity? in (Pütz and Verspoor, 2000, pp. 45–68).

Leshin, R., S.-J. Leslie, and M. Rhodes (2021). Does it matter how we speak about social kinds? A large, preregistered, online experimental study of how language shapes the development of essentialist beliefs. *Child Development 92*, e531–e547.

Levinson, S. (1997). Language and cognition: The cognitive consequences of spatial description in Guugu Yimithirr. *Journal of Linguistic Anthropology 7*, 98–131.

Levinson, S. (2012). Foreword. In (Carroll et al., 2012b, pp. vii–xxiii).

Lévi-Strauss, C. (1951). Language and the analysis of social laws. *American Anthropologist 53*, 155–163.

Liu, L. (1985). Reasoning counterfactually in Chinese: Are there any obstacles? *Cognition 21*, 239–270.

Losonsky, M. (2006). *Linguistic Turns in Modern Philosophy*. Cambridge, UK: Cambridge University Press.

Lucy, J. (1992). *Language Diversity and Thought: A Reformulation of the Linguistic Relativity Hypothesis*. Cambridge, UK: Cambridge University Press.

Lucy, J. (1996). The scope of linguistic relativity: An analysis and review of empirical research. In J. Gumperz and S. Levinson (Eds.), *Rethinking Linguistic Relativity*, pp. 37–69. Cambridge, UK: Cambridge University Press.

Lucy, J. (1997). Linguistic relativity. *Annual Review of Anthropology 26*, 291–312.

Lucy, J. (2010). Language structure, lexical meaning, and cognition: Whorf and Vygotsky revisited. In (Malt and Wolff, 2010, pp. 266286).

Lucy, J. (2016). Recent advances in the study of linguistic relativity in historical context: A critical assessment. *Language Learning 66*, 487–515.

Lucy, J. and S. Gaskins (2001). Grammatical categories and the development of classification preferences: A comparative approach. In (Bowerman and Levinson, 2001, pp. 257–283).

Machery, E. (2024). The replication crisis in embodied cognition research. In L. Shapiro and S. Spaulding (Eds.), *The Routledge Handbook of Embodied Cognition*, 2nd Ed. Oxford: Routledge.

Malotki, E. (1983). *Hopi Time: A Linguistic Analysis of the Temporal Concepts in the Hopi Language*. New York: Mouton.

Malt, B., and P. Wolff (2010). *Words and the Mind: How Words Capture Human Experience*. Oxford, UK: Oxford University Press.

Mandelkern, M. and T. Linzen (2024). Do language models' words refer?

Marchand, J. (1982). Herder, precursor of Humboldt, Whorf, and modern language philosophy. In W. Koepke and S. Knoll (Eds.), *Johann Godfried Herder, Innovator through the Ages*. Bonn: Bouvier.

Martin, L. (1986). Eskimo Words for Snow: A case study in the genesis and decay of an anthropological example. *American Anthropologist 88*, 418–423.

Matolino, B. (2011). Tempels' philosophical racialism. *South African Journal of Philosophy 30*(3), 330–342.

McWhorter, J. (2014). *The Language Hoax: Why the World Looks the Same in Any Language*. New York: Oxford University Press.

Menges, K. (1998). 'Sinn' and 'Besonnenheit': The meaning of 'Meaning' in Herder. *Herder Yearbook 4*, 157–175.

Meßer, D. (2020). Plato's *Cratylus*. In E. N. Zalta (Ed.), *The Stanford Encyclopedia of Philosophy* (Summer 2023 ed.). Metaphysics Research Lab, Stanford University. https://plato.stanford.edu/archives/sum2023/entries/plato-cratylus/.

Metz, T. (2011). Ubuntu as a moral theory and human rights in South Africa. *African Human Rights Law Journal 11*(2), 532–559.

Meyers, W. (1980). *Aliens and Linguists: Language Study and Science Fiction*. Athens: : University of Georgia Press.

Mickan, A., M. Schiefke, and A. Stefanowitsch (2014). Key is a llave is a schlssel: A failure to replicate an experiment from Boroditsky et al. 2003. *Yearbook of the German Cognitive Linguistics Association 2*, 39–50.

Miller, R. L. (1968). *The Linguistic Relativity Principle and Humboldtian Ethnolinguistics*. The Hague: Mouton.

Mithun, M. (1990). Studies of North American Indian languages. *Annual Review of Anthropology 19*, 309–330.

Montemayor, C. (2019). Early and late time perception: On the narrow scope of the Whorfian hypothesis. *Review of Philosophy and Psychology 10*, 133–154.

Mueller-Vollmer, K. and M. Messling (2017). Wilhelm von Humboldt. In E. N. Zalta (Ed.), *The Stanford Encyclopedia of Philosophy*. Metaphysics Research Lab, Stanford University. https://plato.stanford.edu/archives/spr2017/entries/wilhelm-humboldt/.

Müller, F. M. (1887). *The Science of Thought*. New York: Charles Scribner's Sons. Accessed via Google Books https://archive.org/details/sciencethought01mlgoog/mode/2up.

Nater, H. (1984). *The Bella Coola Language*. Ottawa: National Museum of Man; Mercury Series.

Nefdt, R. (2019). The philosophy of linguistics: Scientific underpinnings and methodological disputes. *Philosophy Compass 15*, 1–14.

Nefdt, R. M. (2024). *The Philosophy of Theoretical Linguistics: A Contemporary Outlook*. New York:Cambridge University Press.

Newen, A., L. De Bruin, and S. Gallagher (2018). *The Oxford Handbook of 4E Cognition*. Oxford, UK: Oxford University Press.

Ohmer, X., E. Bruni, and D. Hupkes (2024). From form(s) to meaning: Probing the semantic depths of language models using multisense *Computational Linguistics 50*, 1507–1556.

Papafragou, A., J. Hulbert, and J. Trueswell (2008). Does language guide event perception? Evidence from eye movements. *Cognition 108*, 155–184.

Papafragou, A., P. Li, Y. Choi, and C.-H. Chan (2007). Evidentiality in language and cognition. *Cognition 103*, 253–299.

Pederson, E. (2010). Cognitive linguistics and linguistic relativity. In D. Geeraerts, and H. Cuyckens (Eds.), *The Oxford Handbook of Cognitive Linguistics*, pp. 1012–1044. Oxford, UK: Oxford University Press.

Pederson, E., E. Danzinger, D. Wilkins, S. Levinson, S. Kita, and G. Senft (1998). Semantic typology and spatial conceptualization. *Language 74*, 557–589.

Penn, J. (1972). *Linguistic Relativity versus Innate Ideas*. The Hague: Mouton.

Pike, K. (1954). Emic and Etic standpoints for the description of behavior. In K. Pike (Ed.), *Language in Relation to a Unified Theory of the Structure of Human Behavior*, 2nd Ed., pp. Chapter 2. The Hague: Mouton. Second Edition of the Summer Institute of Linguistics 1954 publication. Accessed via Google Books: https://babel.hathitrust.org/cgi/pt?id=mdp.39015004829167view=1upseq=22skin=2021.

Pinker, S. (1994). *The Language Instinct: The New Science of Language and Mind*. London: Penguin Books.

Pöhls, V. (2013). Testing the untestable? Guidelines for advancing empirical research in the area of Linguistic Relativity. *Rivista Italiana di Filosofia del Linguaggio 7*, 98–108.

Prinz, J. (2020). Culture and Cognitive Science. In E. N. Zalta (Ed.), *The Stanford Encyclopedia of Philosophy* (Summer 2020 ed.). Metaphysics Research Lab, Stanford University. https://plato.stanford.edu/archives/sum2020/entries/culture-cogsci/.

Pullum, G. (1989). The great Eskimo vocabulary hoax. *Natural Language and Linguistic Theory 6*, 579–588. Reprinted in G. Pullum (1991) *The Great Eskimo Vocabulary Hoax, and Other Irreverent Essays on the Study of Language*. Chicago: University of Chicago Press, pp. 579–588.

Pullum, G. (1991). English nominal gerund phrases as noun phrases with verb-phrase heads. *Linguistics 29*, 763–799.

Pullum, G. K. and B. Scholz (2002). Empirical assessment of stimulus poverty arguments. *Linguistic Review 19*, 9–50.

Pütz, M. and M. Verspoor (2000). *Explorations in Linguistic Relativity*. Amsterdam: John Benjamins.

Rambelli, F. (2013). *A Buddhist Theory of Semiotics*. London: Bloomsbury.

Regier, T., P. Kay, A. Gilbert, and R. Ivry (2010). Language and thought: Which side are you on, anyway? In (Malt and Wolff, 2010, 165–182).

Reines, M. and J. Prinz (2009). Reviving Whorf: The return of linguistic relativity. *Philosophy Compass 4*, 1022–1032.

Renard, M. (2021). Reconsidering the language-culture nexus: New Emic insights from Kanien'kéha speakers. Master's thesis, Cambridge University.

Rhodes, M., S.-J. Leslie, L. Bianchi, and L. Chalik (2017). The role of generic language in the early development of social categorization. *Child Development 89*, 148–155.

Rhodes, M., S.-J. Leslie, and C. Tworek (2012). Cultural transmission of social essentialism. *Proceedings of the National Academy of Sciences 109*(34), 13526–13531. DOI: 10.1073/pnas.1208951109

Rhodes, M., S.-J. Leslie, K. Yee, and K. Saunders (2019). Subtle linguistic cues increase girls' engagement in science. *Psychological Science 30*, 455–466.

Ritchie, K. (2021a). Essentializing inferences. *Mind and Language 36*, 570–591.

Ritchie, K. (2021b). Essentializing language and the prospects for ameliorative projects. *Ethics 131*, 460–488.

Roberson, D. and J. Hanley (2010). Relatively speaking: An account of the relationship between language and thought in the color domain. In (Malt and Wolff, 2010, 183–198).

Rorty, R. (Ed.) (1967). *The Linguistic Turn: Essays in Philosophical Method*. Chicago: University of Chicago Press.

Russell, B. (1905). On denoting. *Mind 14*, 479–493.

Russell, B. (1924). Logical atomism. In J. Muirhead (Ed.), *Contemporary British Philosophy*, pp. 356–383. London: Allen & Unwin. Reprinted in B. Russell, *Logic and Knowledge*, London: Allen and Unwin, 1956, pp. 323–343.

Ryle, G. (1953). Ordinary language. *Philosophical Review 62*, 167–186.

Sampson, G. (2013). Gladstone as linguist. *Journal of Literary Semantics 42*, 1–29.

Sapir, E. (1907). On Herder's 'Ursprung der Sprache'. *Modern Philology 5*, 109–142.

Sapir, E. (1916). *Time Perspective in the Aboriginal American Culture, A Study in Method*. Ottawa: Government Printing Bureau.

Sapir, E. (1921). *Language: An Introduction to the Study of Speech*. New York: Harcourt, Brace, & Co. Reprinted paperback 1949.

Sapir, E. (1924). The grammarian and his language. *The American Mercury 1*, 149–155. Accessed through Google Books https://babel.hathitrust.org/cgi/pt?id=mdp.39015030748613&view=1up&seq=3&skin=2021.

Sapir, E. (1927a). Conceptual categories in primitive languages. *Science 74*, 578.
Sapir, E. (1927b). The unconscious patterning of behavior in society. In E. Dummer (Ed.), *The Unconscious: A Symposium*, pp. 114–142. New York: Knopf.
Sapir, E. (1930). *Totality*. Linguistic Society of America. Language Monographs, No. 6.
Sapir, E. (1929). The status of linguistics as a science. *Language 5*, 207–214. Reprinted in David Mandelbaum (ed.), *Selected Writings of Edward Sapir in Language, Culture, and Personality*, pp. 160–166 (Berkeley and Los Angeles: University of California Press, 1968).
Sapir, E. and M. Swadesh (1946). American Indian grammatical categories. *Word 2*, 103–112.
Searle, J. (1980). Minds, brains, and programs. *Behavioral and Brain Sciences 3*, 417–457.
Senft, G. (1997). *Referring to Space: Studies in Austronesian and Papual Languages*. Oxford: Clarendon Press.
Senft, G. (2007). The Nijmegen space games: Studying the interrelationship between language, culture and cognition. In S. Levinson and D. Wilkins (Eds.), *Grammars of Space: Explorations in Cognitive Diversity*, pp. 206–229. Cambridge, UK: Cambridge University Press.
Senft, G. (2017). Absolute frames of spatial reference in Austronesian languages. *Russian Journal of Linguistics 21*, 686–705.
Seuren, P. (1998). *Western Linguistics: An Historical Introduction*. Oxford: Blackwells.
Seuren, P. (2013). *From Whorf to Montague: Explorations in the Theory of Language*. Oxford, UK: Oxford University Press.
Shapiro, L. and S. Spaulding (2024). Embodied Cognition. In E. N. Zalta and U. Nodelman (Eds.), *The Stanford Encyclopedia of Philosophy* (Summer 2024 ed.). Metaphysics Research Lab, Stanford University.
Shaul, D. (1985). Hopi-Raum [review of Malotki (1979,1983)]. *Language 61*, 481–484.
Sidnell, J. and N. J. Enfield (2012). Language diversity and social action: A third locus of linguistic relativity. *Current Anthropology 53*, 302–333.
Sikka, S. (2007). Herder's Critique of Pure Reason. *Review of Metaphysics 61*, 31–50.
Sinha, C. (2012). Cognitive linguistics, psychology and cognitive science. In D. Geeraerts, and G. Cuyckens (Eds.), *The Oxford Handbook of Cognitive Linguistics*, pp. 1266–1294. Oxford, UK: Oxford University Press.
Slobin, D. (1996). From thought and language to thinking for speaking. In J. Gumperz and S. Levinson (Eds.), *Rethinking Linguistic Relativity*, pp. 70–96. Cambridge, UK: Cambridge University Press.
Stam, J. (1980). An historical perspective on linguistic relativity. In R. Rieber (Ed.), *Psychology of Language and Thought*, pp. 239–262. NY: Plenum Press.
Sterken, R. (2019). Linguistic interventions and transformative communicative disruption. In A. Burgess, H. Cappelen, and D. Plunkett (Eds.), *Conceptual Engineering and Conceptual Ethics*, pp. 417–434. Oxford, UK: Oxford University Press.

Swoyer, C. (2015). The linguistic relativity hypothesis. In E. N. Zalta (Ed.), *The Stanford Encyclopedia of Philosophy* (Summer 2015 ed.). Metaphysics Research Lab, Stanford University. https://plato.stanford.edu/archives/sum2015/entries/relativism//supplement2.html. This is Supplement 2 of the earlier entry on "Relativism", available at https://plato.stanford.edu/archives/sum2015/entries/relativism//supplement2.html. The current entry is Baghramian and Carter (2022).

Taylor, C. (2016). *The Language Animal: The Full Shape of the Human Linguistic Capacity*. Cambridge, MA: Harvard University Press.

Tempels, P. (1969). *Bantu Philosophy*. Paris,: Presence africaine.

Thierry, G., P. Athanasopulous, A. Wiggett, B. Dering, and J.-R. Kuipers (2009). Unconscious effects of language-specific terminology on pre-attentive color perception. *Proceedings of the National Academy of Sciences 106*, 4567–4570.

Trabant, J. (2000). How relativistic are Humboldt's "Weltansichten"? In (Pütz and Verspoor, 2000, pp. 25–44).

Trier, J. (1932). Sprachliche Felder. *Zeitschrift für die Bedeutungslehre 8*, 417–427.

van Eijk, J. and T. Hess (1986). Noun and verb in Salish. *Lingua 69*, 319–331.

Vaswani, A., N. Shazeer, N. Parmar, J. Uszkoreit, L. Jones, A. Gomez, Ł. Kaiser, and I. Polosukhin (2017). Attention is all you need. In I. Guyon *et al* (Ed.), *Advances in Neural Information Processing Systems, 30*, Volume 30. Curran Associates, Inc.

Vendler, Z. (1971). Summary: Linguistics and the a priori. In Z. Vendler (Ed.), *Philosophy and Linguistics*, pp. 245–265. London: Macmillan Education UK.

Voegelin, C. and Z. Harris (1945). Index to the Franz Boas collection of materials for American linguistics. *Language 21*(3), 5–43.

von Humboldt, W. (1836). *On Language: The Diversity of Human Language-Structure and its Influence on the Mental Development of Mankind*. Cambridge, UK: Cambridge University Press. Translated by Peter Heath, with a very long and informative Introduction by Hans Aarseleff. This work was initially published 1836 as *Über die Verscheidenheitdes menschlichen Sprachbaues und ihren Einflußauf die geistige Entwickelung des Menschengeschlechts*, having prior to that been the Introductory essay to the three-volume work by Humboldt, *On the Kawi Language on the Island of Java*.

von Humboldt, W. (1997). *Essays on Language*. Frankfurt: P. Lang. Volume edited by T. Harden and D. Farrelly.

Weisgerber, L. (1949). *Die Sprache unter den Kräften des menschlichen Daseins (Language among the Powers of Human Existence)*. Düsseldorf: Schwann.

Weisgerber, L. (1950). *Vom Weltbild der deutschen Sprache (The World View of the German Language)*. Düsseldorf: Schwann.

Weissbach, M. M. (1999). Wilhelm von Humboldt's study of the Kawi language: The proof of the existence of the Malayan-Polynesian language culture. *Fidelio 8/1*. HTML and PDF versions are available at https://archive.schillerinstitute.com/fidelio_archive/1999/fidv08n01-1999Sp/index.html.

Whitney, W. D. (1875). *The Life and Growth of Language*. New York & London: D. Appleton. Accessed through Google Books https://books.google.ca/books/about/The_Life_and_Growth_of_Language.html?id=81gsAAAAMAAJ&redir_esc=y.

Whorf, B. (1932). A central Mexican inscription combining Mexican and Maya day signs. *American Anthropology 34*, 296–302. Reprinted in (Carroll, 1956b, pp. 43–50); (Carroll et al., 2012, pp. 55–64).

Whorf, B. (1938). The Yale report. First appeared in Lee (1996); reprinted in (Carroll et al., 2012, pp. 345–376).

Whorf, B. (1940a). Linguistics as an exact science. *Technology Review 43*, 62–63, 80–83. Reprinted in (Carroll et al., 2012, pp. 281–298); (Carroll, 1956b, pp. 220–232).

Whorf, B. (1940b). Science and linguistics. *Technology Review 42*, 229–231, 247–248. Reprinted in (Carroll et al., 2012, pp. 265–280); (Carroll, 1956b, pp. 207–219).

Whorf, B. (1941a). Languages and logic. *Technology Review 43*, 250–252, 266, 268, 272. Reprinted in (Carroll et al., 2012, pp. 299–314); (Carroll, 1956b, pp. 233–245).

Whorf, B. (1941b). The relation of habitual thought and behavior to language. In L. Spier, A. Hallowell, and S. Newman (Eds.), *Language, Culture, and Personality: Essays in Memory of Edward Sapir*, pp. 75–93. Sapir Memorial Publication Fund (1st Ed; Reprinted Univ. Utah Press, Salt Lake City, 1960.). Reprinted in (Carroll et al., 2012, pp. 173–204); (Carroll, 1956b, pp 134–159). This paper is sometimes referred to as "Whorf's Sapir Memorial paper".

Whorf, B. (1942). Language, mind, and reality. Reprinted in (Carroll et al., 2012, pp. 315–344); (Carroll, 1956b, pp. 246–270).

Whorf, B. (1945). Grammatical categories. *Language 21*, 1–11. Reprinted in (Carroll et al., 2012, pp. 113–130); (Carroll, 1956b, pp. 87–101). Carroll's footnote on the first page of each reprinted version remarks that it was "written in late 1937 at the request of Franz Boas, then editor of the *International Journal of American Linguistics*, The manuscript was found in the Boas collection by C.F. Voegelin and Z.S. Harris." The complete list of the Boas collection makes up the totality of *Language* v. 21, no. 3; 1945. This item of Whorf's is listed under Hopi.

Whorf, B. (1946). The Milpa Alta dialect of Aztec, with notes on the Classical and the Tepoztlán dialects. In (Hoijer, 1946, pp. 367–387).

Whorf, B. (1950). An American Indian model of the universe. *International Journal of American Linguistics 16*, 67–72. Reprinted in (Carroll et al., 2012, pp. 73–82); (Carroll, 1956b, pp. 57–64).

Whorf, B. (1952). *Collected Papers on Metalinguistics*, 2nd Ed. Washington, DC: Foreign Service Institute, USA Department of State. The 1st Edition was published in 1949 under the title *Four Articles on Metalinguistics*. The four articles were Whorf (1940b,a, 1941a,b). The 2nd Edition added Whorf (1950).

Williamson, T. (2007). *The Philosophy of Philosophy*. Malden, MA: Wiley-Blackwell.

Winawer, J., N. Witthoft, M. Frank, L. Wu, A. Wade, and L. Boroditsky (2007). Russian blues reveal effects of language on color discrimination. *Proceedings of the National Academy of Science 104*, 7780–7785.

Wiredu, K. (1985). The concept of truth in the Akan language. In P. O. Bodunrin (Ed.), *Philosophy in Africa: Trends and Perspectives*, pp. 236–239 University of Ife Press.

Wittgenstein, L. (1953). *Philosophical Investigations*. New York, NY, USA: Wiley-Blackwell.

Wodak, D., S.-J. Leslie, and M. Rhodes (2015). What a loaded generalization: Generics and social cognition. *Philosophy Compass 10*, 625–635.

Wolff, P. and K. Holmes (2011). Linguistic relativity. *Wiley Interdisciplinary Reviews: Cognitive Science 2*, 253–265.

Wu, C. (1994). *"If Triangles Were Circles...": - A Study of Counterfactuals in Chinese and English*. Taipei: Crane Publishing.

Yeh, D. and D. Gentner (2005). Reasoning counterfactually in Chinese: Picking up the pieces. In B. Bara, L. Barsalou, and M. Bucciarelli (Eds.), *Proceedings of the 27th Annual Meeting of the Cognitive Science Society*, Volume 27, Mahwah, pp. 2410–2415. Cognitive Science Society: Lawrence Erlbaum.

Yun, H. and S. Choi (2018). Spatial semantics, cognition, and their interaction: A comparative study of spatial categorization in English and Korean. *Cognitive Science 42*, 1736–1776.

Index

A
African philosophy 92, 96, 100, 102, 130
Akan 100–2
analytic philosophy 92–3, 94, 96, 102
Apache 41, 52
artificial intelligence 92, 119–24, 132

B
Bach, E. 63, 65–6, 102–3
Baffin Island 19–20
Bantu 68, 100
Basque 15
Bender, E. 121–3
Berlin Academy Prize 9, 30
bilingualism 53, 83
Boas, F. 6, 7, 19–31, 42, 46, 78, 128

C
Canadian Geological Survey 32
categorization 61, 69, 76–7, 88
ChatGPT 116, 120, 122
Chinese 15, 62, 89
Chinese room 120–1
Chomsky, N. 13, 15, 48, 62, 103–7, 110, 125
Chomskyan linguistics 8, 103, 131
Clark, R. 8, 13, 20, 116
classification 21–2, 51
cognitive linguistics 48, 92, 109–11, 116–19, 123, 131
Cognitive Science 90–124
color 21, 68, 70–8, 81–2, 89, 94, 100, 124
computational theory of mind 110–1
conceptual engineering 85–6, 99
construction grammar 109, 112
counterfactual reasoning 89
covert category 24, 43, 46–7
critical period 6, 9, 48–9

Cylons 119

D
Deutscher, G. 8, 50, 82

E
Edwards, R. 39, 41–2
embodied cognition and 4E approaches 92, 110, 115–9
emic and etic views 2–3, 49, 59, 66, 69–70, 80–82, 95, 129
evolution 9, 20–1, 107, 112

F
faculty of language 105, 107
Frege, G. 93–4, 121

G
genetic problem 51–2
Greenberg, J. 27, 39, 59–61
Guugu Yimithirr 82

H
habitual Whorfianism 129
Hamann, J. 8, 11, 18
Henry, J. 30, 60, 61
Herder, J. 6, 8–13, 18, 25–30, 127
Hoijer, H. 27, 33, 42, 59–60, 67, 70, 128
Homer 11, 81–2
Hopi 2, 41–2, 49–60, 63, 78, 83, 91, 126
Humboldt, Alexander von 14, 128
Humboldt, Wilhelm von 6, 14–5, 128

I
Inuit *see also* (*snow, Inuit words for*) 19–20, 118

J
Johnson, M. 113–6

K
kaleidoscopic 43, 126
Kant 6, 8-9, 11-12, 48, 93, 125, 127
Kawi 15-16
Korean 71, 88

L
Láadan (artificial language) 90
language reform 84
large language models 92, 119, 121
Levinson, S. 1, 50-51, 82, 108, 130
linguistic anthropology 14, 48, 131
linguistic turn in philosophy 92-4, 96, 99, 102, 131

M
Malagasy 109
Malotki, E. 49, 52-3, 56-9, 126
Mandarin 62, 84, 114-15, 120
Martin, L. 22-3, 76
mass vs. count nouns 2, 54-5, 79, 129
Mayan 40-1, 51
metaphor 56-8, 68, 84, 113-4, 117
modularity thesis 106, 110

N
Naquayouma 41-2, 45, 53
Newspeak 89
Nootka 32, 52, 63-5
numbers and counting 60, 107, 116, 118, 122

O
octopus cognition 117, 121-2, 124
oligosynthesis 40
overt category 46

P
perception 11, 45, 76-7, 79, 88, 106, 116
phonetic/phoneme 22, 30-1, 81
Pinker, S. 49-50, 52
polysynthetic languages 62, 66
principles and parameters framework 62, 104-5
psychology experiments 67-8, 71, 75, 80-7, 91, 114-5, 118, 129
Pullum, G. 23, 105, 109

R
recursion 106-7

Rorty, R. 93-4, 96
Russell, B. 27, 44, 93-4, 96-7
Ryle, G. 97-99

S
Salishan 65
science fiction 89-1, 106, 131
Seuren, P. 130
Shawnee 52
snow, Inuit words for see also (vocabulary hoax) 22-23, 123
Southern Paiute 31
space and time
    directions 49, 82, 83
    events 57-8, 90, 113
    spatial conceptualization 56, 74-5, 82, 84, 88
    spatio-temporal conceptualization 56-7, 84
    temporal conceptualization 12, 56-7, 58, 84, 115
Swadish, M. 33-4, 62

T
The Undergraduate Disease 3, 91
translation 16, 18, 40, 49, 53-5, 58-61, 63-4, 73, 81-2, 109, 120, 126, 129
types of relativism
    global linguistic 74, 76
    grand 80, 89, 91, 115, 129
    medial 80, 83, 91, 100, 107, 115
    minor 79-80, 86, 91, 94

U
Uto-Aztecan 51

V
verbal interference 75
viewpoint 6, 12, 19, 69, 88, 128
vocabulary hoax see (snow, Inuit words for) 23

W
Williamson, T. 93-4, 96
Wittgenstein, L. 93-5, 97, 121
Wuwtsim 53, 58

Y
Yana 30-1